Lady of All Nations

The Apparitions of the Blessed Virgin

Mohamed el-Fers

ISBN 978-1-4092-9525-9
Lady of all Nations
The Apparitions of the Blessed Virgin
2

Simultaneously in Fatima and Amsterdam

Ida is just twelve years old when a beautiful Lady in a dazzling light appears to her. The child immediately recognizes her as the Blessed Virgin, clad in a long white dress with a cream-colored sash.

She is pregnant and just smiles at the child that is basking in Her light.

That very same day and hour in Fatima, the last of six separate sightings of Maria apparitions takes place.

The children of Fatima and Ida see a *bilocate* apparition.

That the Amsterdam Apparitions received approval with the consent of Benedict XVI, then Cardinal Ratzinger, and the acceptance of the late John Paul II in 2002, is just one of the many miracles foretold by that Lady.

The magic formula the Blessed Virgin gave in Amsterdam is believed to be capable of saving the church and the world.

It is furthered believed that intervening in such a prayer is not unlike the work of Satan.

Even more so since it all happened after the apparition was approved.

But it cannot be, as the interference and intervention in the Amsterdam Blessing was done by the Vatican by a less high ranking official.

So it merely demonstrates the enormous importance of this prayer.

Although Archbishop Amato and Cardinal William Levada both contributed to the fact that there are now three different Amsterdam Blessings in circulation, it was Angelo Amato who initiated the way most Catholics now utter this formula.

They are either silent or say 'the Holy Virgin Mary' or 'that once was Mary'.

The Levada version is used only when the Amsterdam Blessing is said in the presence of church officials.

Our Lady of Amsterdam came a long way. But Amsterdam is no Fatima. Ida Peerdeman is told to keep quiet.

She has been regarded as hysteric for decades, and not only in ecclesiastical circles, because Mary appeared to her.

Even the Catholic press demonized Ida and her Apparitions. But with the rise of Spiritualism there is an increase in popular interest in the supernatural.

Although each request for an interview was rejected, in the early 60s a program was arranged for Ida at the KRO, the Catholic Broadcast Federation.

Dutch Television was still in its infancy, with only one black and white channel.

In those days not everyone could afford a TV-set. But there were hordes of spectators in cafes and halls.

The streets were deserted as Catholics and Protestants alike flocked together to watch the Amsterdam Bernadette.

Ida appeared on TV with express permission of the bishop.

"And when did She appear?"

Ida recalled the number of times and the dates, oblivious to the fact that she is being interrogated like some criminal.

Ida: *"They put me on the show with a black box over my eyes."*

None their questions showed any sympathy to her case.

Ida: *"They treated me like I was hysterical, some kind of mad woman."*

Ida resolutely refused to grant anymore interviews after this experience, which she also did when I asked her.

Ida: *"You need to apply for permission to the bishop. But he will refuse, I can tell you right now. And without his consent, I may not speak."*

Why?

"Well, they assume all I'm doing is to try and make myself look interesting. They say nasty, villainous, and dirty things about me."

But aren't you free to speak to whoever you like?

"Yes, but not when it comes to the press. Sometimes that was difficult, of course.

I can understand these reporters, the fact that they do their work: searching for and digging up news. That is what a journalist is for.

But I dare not speak. For the last fifty years I thought: please let me be obedient and keep silent."

But you won't be alive much longer, and then no one will know your own story ...

"No, then I'll be gone."

Shortly before Ida Peerdeman died, she agreed to do an interview with me.

On condition that I only publish it after her death. We came to an agreement on April 20, 1996.

Two days later, I called her again. This time she even seemed eager to talk.

I felt like a chosen one. Ida spoke freely with me for two long evenings. I consider myself blessed to be have been able to speak with her.

About her youth, her life, her fears. How she was treated when people found out what had appeared to her.

I was privileged to speak with the woman who in a few years time would officially be recognized as someone who had seen the Holy Virgin, who millions of Catholics all over the world regarded to be destined for sainthood.

And Ida did not mince her words: "*I've said things I've never said to anybody before. I hope you will not use it against me.*"

Alkmaar 1905

For weeks, the little Gesina Peerdeman let everybody know that she wanted to have a doll for her birthday present. On her birthday, her father Rembert took her to the bedroom, where her mother Lena showed her the newborn Ida.

"Isn't she a beautiful doll?"

Gesina looks into the cradle and stamps her feet:

"I don't want a doll like that! I want a real doll!, she cries insulted.

Ida was the youngest daughter in a family of five children. She is baptized Isje Johanna by Father H.A. Horning in the parish church in Alkmaar on the same day she was born, August 13, 1905.

Ida is five years old when the family moved to the center of Amsterdam Center at Langestraat 18. They lived on the first floor apartment until 1935.

Three years later. It is July 1914. The Black Month as it will be called. The assassination of Archduke Franz Ferdinand in Sarajevo triggers the First World War.

A tragic month for the Peerdeman-family too, as both mother and child die during childbirth. It is July 18, 1914.

Her mother Helena was only thirty-five years old. Ida is eight.

Hard times! Her father has to travel all over the Netherlands to make a living as a textile merchant. In his absence, the then 16-year-old Gesina looks after her three little sisters and brother. She cooks, she cleans, she does everything a mother would have done. She would love to work as a nurse, day-dreaming that one day a nice Catholic doctor will discover her and ask for her hand.

Gesina would have accept any decent proposal of marriage that could take her away from this misery in this first year of World War I.

But Gesina is desperately needed at home.

The Catholic family is not considered particularly pious. They would go to the nearby Dominican church on Sundays. "*We said a prayer at the dinner table, but that is all*", Ida would later recall.

In those days the local chaplain was a regular visitor at their home. In this case the Dominican Father Frehe.

Ida: "*Yes, I think they had sent him to offer our family a little help. My father and Father Frehe hit it off right from the start, the two had the same sense of humor.*"

After two years of high school, Ida decided she wanted to become a kindergarten teacher, just like her sister Truus.

But after a practical lesson with children, she is sent home by her teacher who told her.: "Unfortunately, you are not suitable. You lack the imagination that is such an indispensable element in fulfilling this task.

This comment as to her total lack of imagination, was to prove favourable to her later on in her life, when questions were raised regarding the veracity of her testimony about the apparitions of the Blessed Virgin in Amsterdam.

Disappointed, in 1921 Ida takes a job as the youngest employee in the administration department of the perfume company Boldoot.

The office is near her house, in fact just around the corner. The production plant is on the westside of the city at Haarlemmerweg.

As a child Ida was not at all 'Marian' but felt more of an affinity for the husband of Our Lady, Saint Joseph.

And then, on Saturday, October 13, 1917, Our Lady appeared for the very first time in Amsterdam. The same day and same hour the Holy Virgin was seen in Fatima, a small village in Portugal.

Ida is on her way back home after taking confession in the Dominican church in the Amsterdam Spuistraat. At the end of the street she is overwhelmed by a brilliant gleaming light. In this light she sees a lady.

"She was dressed in a long white robe and a veil, her arms slightly spread, and a lovely, friendly smile. She looked like a very beautiful Jewish girl."

Ida had never seen anything as beautiful in her entire life. This can only be the Holy Virgin, she thought.

The Lady gives her a friendly nod before she disappears.

Ida runs home. Her father tells her not to talk about it with anyone: "People would think that you're crazy and ridicule you. That is the last thing we need!"

Ida's confidant Father Frehe, also learned of the extraordinary event. He too gives her the advice to keep everything to herself.

In Fatima, Portugal it was a farewell that day. In Amsterdam the beautiful Lady in dazzling light made a second and third appearance that October in 1917.

When Ida talks about it at home, only her brother Piet is interested. When the Lady of all Peoples makes her appearance again many years later, Ida immediately recognizes her as the same Lady in White.

It is thirty-three years later, during the twenty-fifth officially recognized appearance as Mother of all Nations, that Ida asks the apparition:

"*Will they believe me?*"

It is then Our Lady reminds Ida of her three previous apparitions in 1917, and speaks:

"Yes. That is why I came to you earlier, when you did not understand. That was not necessary at that time, but now it is proof." (December 10, 1950).

As a young girl, Ida had many admirers, but increasingly she began suffering from demonic attacks.

During a walk through the city twenty-year-old Ida is hounded by a big man, all dressed in black.

"Black, like a priest."

The Amsterdam canal where Satan tried to drown Ida.

His penetrating gaze disturbed her. Ida tries to get away from him and starts walking faster.

The man in black is catches her. He suddenly tries to grab her by the arm and drag her into a canal to drown her.

In the desperate fight for her life, a soft voice sounds.

The black guy loosens his grip with an odious cry, leaves her and disappears.

From that day on, Gesina was ordered by father to bring her youngest sister to her daily work and retrieval her in the evening.

They meet again this sinister black guy. He gives a smile, but dares not to touch Ida now Gesina is with her.

When the girl is attacked for the third time, the creature is disguised as a frail old woman. Who claims to know Ida from the church.

She gives the girl an address and invites her to come along soon.

Ida turns down the invitation, but agrees to assist the old lady crossing the street.

Half way the street-crossing, she recognized the eyes. It is the black guy again. A crippling fear suddenly comes over her.

With an iron grip he takes her arm again and drags her in front of an approaching tram.

Ida cried. Just in time the tramway brakes. The creature loose his grip and disappeared.

Brother Piet, together with the fiancé of her sister Jo, go to find the address reported by the old woman. It is an old, empty house.

If the Borley Rectory is *the most haunted house in England*, the Langestraat 18 most certain is its Amsterdam equal. When Ida comes home, it looks that she enters the set of a Poltergeist movie.

The word is from poltern, meaning to rumble, and Geist, meaning "ghost" in German. It denotes an invisible spirit that manifests itself by moving and influencing objects.

The evidence is anecdotal, and given by the sisters of Ida to the parents of Herman Brouwer, the late chairman of the Lady of all Peoples Foundation.

Or told by the brother of Ida, who informed his daughter Helena, who passed the word to the Austrian priest Father Paul Sigl.

It is hardly surprising that some of the stories about this period of Ida's life have several versions.

Ida as a 19-year-old secretary was seemingly the unwitting cause of much chaos. At home as well as on the job weird things were going on when she was around, including disruption of electricity and telephone lines, swinging lamps and strange sounds. The effects moved with the young Ida when she changed from the office to the plant at the Haarlemmerweg. Here the polter faded only, after Ida had an heart attack.

But at home lamps are swinging wildly back and forth. Doors opened and closed automatically. The hands of the clock are running around like crazy. The oven, rarely used, began to smoke by itself. Raspy voices and noises are heard, such as cackling, tapping and footsteps. And chairs move around.

One day Ida is quietly reading the Sursum Corda on the stair leading to the 1st floor, as she is knocked down by an unknown force.

The place where this happened on the stair was for years to come known as a cold spot.

The Peerdeman family lived on the first floor of the right house on the picture.

Some skeptics propose that all poltergeist activity untraceable to fraud has a physical explanation. The theory is not complete, however, because it accounts for the movement of objects but not for the strange voices and effects displayed in the case of the Amsterdam Apparitions.

When Ida is attacked by demons the whole family suffers with her.

When father Frehe in his presbytery is preparing to pay a visit to the Peerdeman family, Ida starts at the same time cursing in rage.

She suddenly have such great physical strength, that she lift the a heavy chair above her head. Her voice is totally changed.

Within Catholicism is not uncommon that a future saint first undergoes such possession, before she is ready to receive a great mercy.

Something like what Ida experienced, we know from the life of the holy Carmelite Abellin of Mirjam (Mirjam Baouardi).

This Arab Saint, born in 1846 in the village of Abellin near Nazareth in Palestine, had undergone like Ida the strangest horrors.

They were not just imaginations and certainly not fancy. The whole family Peerdeman witness strange moves and sounds.

The help of Father Frehe is invoked.

First he tells Ida's father to give minimal attention to this demonic tormentor.

After a while you will get used to it that the door-bell suddenly without stop starts to ring. That all cupboard doors opening on their own, the hands of the clock turning at a dizzying speed, electrical fuses blew out and the lamp in the living room suddenly start its wild swing.

Often, when the Polter starts, father Peerdeman jocular remarks: "Come all in. The more souls, the more joy."

The intrepid nature of father Peerdeman is a huge support for the children. They all do their best to ignore the creepy events.

Ida: *"Thanks to my father, we all had a pleasant, homely and happy childhood. He was always with us to the church. At home we made music and sung. Father and my sisters played piano, my brother and I violin."*

If the Polter hits particularly hard, the family would talk themselves into courage with a significant: *"Come on guys, smile! Because if we do not laugh, then the devils do it, and that we do not give pleasure!"*

Just pretend nothing was going on.

But how can you ignore when Ida is attacked by the dark power in her own living room. As an invisible hand is trying to strangle her.

When those diabolical manifestations were growing heavier, Father Frehe acknowledges that Ida was victim of the devil's tyranny. Frehe asked the bishop's permission to perform exorcism.

Author Robert Lemm: "*The devil had long been aware that Ida would be chosen by Mary to bear Her message throughout the world.*"

The New Testament includes exorcism among the miracles performed by Jesus. Because of this precedent, demonic possession was part of the belief system of Christianity since its beginning, and exorcism is still a recognized practice of Catholicism. But the Anglican Church also has an official exorcist in each diocese.

Solemn exorcisms, according to the Canon law of the Roman Catholic church, can be exercised only by an ordained priest or higher prelate, with the express permission of the local bishop, and only after a careful medical examination to exclude the possibility of mental illness.

Things listed in the Roman Ritual as being indicators of possible demonic possession include: speaking foreign or ancient languages of which the possessed has no prior knowledge; supernatural abilities and strength; knowledge of hidden or remote things which the possessed has no way of knowing, an aversion to anything holy, profuse blasphemy, and sacrilege.

After Ida is checked by the docter the bishop's permission is given, Father Frehe performed an exorcism in the living room.

The act of exorcism is considered to be an incredibly dangerous spiritual task. The ritual assumes that the possessed Ida retain her free will, though the demon may hold control over her physical body.

Ida as a possessed person is not regarded as evil in herself, nor wholly responsible for her actions.

Frehe used the Benedictine Vade retro satana and relics, invokes several different saints and archangels. And all strange manifestations seems to occur at once.

At the end of a long and exhausting session Satan speaks to Frehe with a voice of his own.

The last thing the devil said to him was: "You priests, I will get even with you!"

On the way back to his residence, Father Frehe fell through a metal grate. He barely survived it.

But the exorcism was performed quit well. Until the beginning of May 1940 Ida's life was relatively quiet.

Jo is the only one of the Peerdeman-sisters that will marry.

They are so happy for her when she becomes Mrs. Johanna Groothues Heidkamp-Peerdeman.

But her good-looking husband is often abroad due to his work for a British Road Construction Company. Not for days, but sometimes months.

When he is assigned for a year to a prolonged job in South Africa, Jo will follow suit to be with her husband.

A few weeks before the planned leave, a telegram arrives from KwaZulu-Natal, South Africa.

It says in a few words that her husband is dead.

Later a letter arrives with a little more details. Not what caused his death, but that Jos man is buried on a cemetery not far from the Durban Road he was working on.

The conditions of his death are never clarified. Most likely he was one of the many victims of a robbery.

May 1940 an astonishing event took place: Ida had visions dealing in detail with the unfolding of the battle in Europe.

She saw Mussolini being hung from his feet four years in advance. Could give detailed descriptions of what was going on in Hitler's Eagles Nest on the top of the Berchtesgaden mountain.

When she received these visions, her gaze was fixed and she expressed what she was hearing and seeing very slowly to the people around her.

The war visions end on March 25, 1945, when the Lady she had seen in 1917 once again appeared.

Ida is now forty, unmarried, living with her sisters and still doing clerical work for the perfume factory of Boldoot.

Like any of the working woman, arising every morning and returning in the evening.

Yet heaven opened.

The first apparition of Mary as the Lady of all Peoples took place on March 25, 1945, the Feast of the Annunciation. Her coming was an event that occurred in all silence and simplicity, hidden from the eyes of the world.

In that year the Annunciation coincided with Palm Sunday. World War II was still going on in the Netherlands, and Amsterdam was living through a horrible period in its history.

Ida and her three sisters were at home, seated around a pot-bellied stove. Father Frehe, who was transferred to Alkmaar, stopped by for a visit.

While they were engaged in lively conversation, something extraordinary happened.

Ida noticed something in the adjoining room. She got up and saw that immense light she saw the first time in October 1917 appeared again.

Ida's recount of that March 25, 1945, the Feast of the Annunciation:

"My sisters and I sat talking in the drawing-room, around the pot-bellied stove. The war was still going on, and it was the time of the 'hunger-winter'. Father Frehe was in town that day and stopped by for a brief visit. We were in deep conversation when, all at once, I felt drawn to the adjoining room and suddenly saw a light appearing there. I got up and couldn't help going towards it. The wall disappeared before my eyes, and with it everything that had been there. It was one sea of light and an infinite depth."

As her surroundings seemed to fade away, the same girl dressed in white Ida had seen in October 1917 come forth.

"She was standing with her arms lowered and the palms of her hands turned outwards, towards me."

But this time the Lady, all at once, began to speak to Ida, saying:

"Repeat after me."

The Lady speaks very slowly and Ida repeat after her, word-for-word.

"She raises first three, then four and finally five fingers, while telling me: The 3 is March, the 4 is April and the 5 is May 5th."

At that moment Ida doesn't understand. Why the Lady tells her the numbers of the months? Or isn't she?

The 5th of May is since than celebrated as National Holyday every year. Our Lady predicts the liberation of the Netherlands on May 5, 1945.

Then the Lady shows Ida that she has a Rosary with her and says:

"It is thanks to this. Persevere!"

She waits a little, and then says:

"The prayer must be spread."

Then Ida got a vision like Jesus himself had a vision. Jesus' baptism by John is concluded by images of the heavens opening the dove-like descent of the Holy Spirit and a heavenly voice.

Ida's visions comprise inspirational renderings of the future.

Ida: "I see nothing but soldiers in front of me, many Allies, and the Blessed Virgin points at them" with the crucifix of the Rosary to tell her that the troops will soon go home.

Ida's sisters and Fr. Frehe had gathered around her. When Frehe heard her speaking, he said to one of the sisters, "Just write down what she says." After Ida had repeated a couple of sentences, she heard him say: "Listen, just ask who it is."

Ida ask: "Are you Mary?"

The figure smiles at her and answers,

"They will call me *The Lady... Mother*."

The image fades away very slowly before Ida's eyes. A cross is laid down before her and Ida is asked to take it up.

Ida: "I take it up very slowly, and it is heavy... Only then did the light also go away, and all at once I saw everything around me in the room as it had always been."

This was the first of a series of fifty-six apparitions over the course of fourteen years. The majestic last farewell apparition would take place fourteen years later, on Sunday May 31, 1959.

It was almost three o'clock afternoon when Ida, gathered with friends and family in the living room saw suddenly something happening in the air outside the window.

Startled she said: "Look there!" as she pointed at the sky. All go to the window, and Ida sees a tremendous light over the Wandelweg. She could not look into it and covered her eyes with her hands. All the others did not see anything strange, so they asked Ida what was happening. Ida knelt down and folded her hands.

Ida: "Yet I was compelled to look at it. While looking at it, I thought that the sky was being torn apart. What I saw was really a tearing apart of the sky."

Then suddenly she saw the Lady in all her glory, but without the sheep, globe and Cross as she was depicted by Heinrich Repke from Germany.

Ida: "Never before had I seen her like that… I only saw the Lady, but with an immense splendor of light and glory about her. Then I suddenly had to look at her head, and I saw that now she was wearing a crown. This I had never seen before. I didn't see a crown with diamonds or of gold, yet I knew that it was a crown, sparkling with light on all sides, more beautiful than the most beautiful diamond crown. Moreover, the Lady herself was one blaze of light."

Ida saw a piece of thin, blue sky and, beneath it, the upper part of the globe. It was completely black. This gave her "a terribly sad and ghastly impression".

On this last Amsterdam Apparition Ida noticed that the Lady is waving her finger continuously to and fro and shaking her head—as if in disapproval and warning—at that black world.

Then she heard the Blessed Virgin saying:

"Do penance."

From out of the dark, black globe Ida saw all sorts of human heads emerging. She saw them rising slowly upward, then their bodies, and finally she saw those people whole and entire, standing upon the round hemisphere.

Ida: "I thought: how is it possible that there are so many different races and sorts of people?"

As she looked on in amazement at all those people, she saw the Lady extending her hands in blessing over those people, and then she no longer looked so sad.

Then she heard:

"Make reparation to Him."

And suddenly the Amsterdam Madonna was gone.

In place of her Ida had the most peculiar visions. She sees an incredibly large Host. Then in front of the Host appeared a large chalice of splendid gold, toppled over, with the opening towards Ida.

From the chalice she saw thick streams of blood flowing upon the globe and streamed down from the earth.

Ida: "It was a very distressing sight; it made me feel quite sick."

The streams of blood went on for quite a while, when suddenly all of that was transformed. Everything became a dazzling Holy Host like white fire, with such a brilliant light emanated from it that Ida had to cover her eyes again with her hands. Although she feared to go blind, "inwardly" she was forced to look at it.

In its center the Holy Host was a little opening or hollow. All of a sudden the Host burst open and Ida saw a floating figure emerging from it, a Person, so mighty, so majestic that Ida cannot convey the majesty and might which was emanating from this figure. It was too overwhelming for her and she hardly dared to look.

But she did look at that mighty and majestic Figure!

Ida: "I felt within me very strongly: it is the Lord."

This is so unique and one can understand why this was saved for the very last of the Amsterdam Apparitions!

Ida, while facing The Lord: "I felt myself so terribly small compared to that indescribable majesty. A kind of cloth was wrapped around His body—over His shoulders and then slanting down around His body. His face was shining incredibly. His feet were placed one upon the other, as you sometimes see on a crucifix. On His feet I saw a scar, from which beams of light were coming forth. His hands were a bit raised, one hand somewhat higher than the other. In His hands, too, I saw some kind of scars. From them as well, great beams of light were coming forth. I saw one Person, but all the while I kept thinking: and yet there are two. But when I looked, I saw only one. Still, it kept going through my head: and yet there are two.

Then all at once an indescribable light came from out of their midst, and in it I saw, coming forth from their midst—I cannot express it otherwise—a Dove going down to the globe as fast as an arrow. Going ahead of that dove was an indescribable light and, behind it, an enormous bunch of rays. That light was so immense that, once again, I couldn't look into it and had to cover my eyes with my hands. My eyes were hurting from it. Again, however, I was forced to look. What glory and what power were shining forth from it all: that floating Figure, majestic, mighty, grand; and then that light with the now brightly illuminated world."

Then Ida heard the common words said in the Mass after the communion: Whoever eats and drinks Me acquires eternal life and receives the True Spirit.

Then the Lady came back again in all her glory, exactly as at the beginning.

Ida: "Now, however, I very clearly saw the difference between her glory, if I may express it this way, and the great power and majesty of the floating Figure. It was as if the Lady were standing in the shadow of the Lord—that was the feeling which came over me.

Now the Lady looked happy. She looked at me full of love, and I heard her say very softly, from afar,

"Farewell."

And then very softly she added,

"See you in Heaven."

Ida's sisters, as usually present during the apparitions, the eldest would note down the words Ida would repeat after the Blessed Virgin.

But this time, this last apparition, made Ida so sad that she could no longer repeat the last words, as she began to cry.

She felt that this was the departure, for good. Our Lady of Amsterdam very slowly disappears and then the light goes off.

The many messages that Ida had received concern the spiritual state of the Church and the faithful, with many warnings for the brood of vipers and prophecies which clearly predict the political and spiritual turbulence to come.

Now, more than fifty years later, this all the more remarkable, many of the prophesies have been fulfilled: the founding of the Jewish state of Israel, the Cold War, the first landing on the moon, AIDS, the Balkan war, the downfall of communism, the economic crises and many more. It is with good reason that the Lady says, "It will come true thought the years" and "The signs are in my words".

Following the proclamation of the dogma of the Assumption of Mary into Heaven on November 1, 1950, the messages take on a new direction.

The great plan by which the Lady wishes to save the world, gradually unfolds.

On February 11, 1951, Mary delivered a special prayer, the Amsterdam Blessing, to be spread throughout the whole world.

If said, consequently, it will bring about a completely new outpouring of the Holy Spirit and "corruption, disaster and war" will progressively diminish.

Lord Jesus Christ, Son of the Father,

send now Your Spirit over the earth.

Let the Holy Spirit live in the hearts of all nations,

that they may be preserved

from degeneration, disasters, and war.

May the Lady of all Nations,

who once was Mary,

be our Advocate,

Amen.

The Lady promises to help the world, and announces the coming of a new Spirit, a white Dove Who will send forth His rays.

"I place my foot on the world. I will help them and lead them to the goal, but they must listen…"

On March 4, 1951 the Lady says:

"Now imprint this clearly on your memory: I am standing on the globe and both my feet are firmly fixed upon it. You can also see clearly my hands, my face, my hair, and my veil. The rest is as though in a haze... Have this picture of me painted and together with it, spread the prayer I have taught you... I want to be 'The Lady of all Peoples' and, therefore, I require of you to get the prayer translated into all the principal languages and said every day."

It was father Frehe that introduced the seer to the Brenninkmeijer-family in Amsterdam. The Brenninkmeijer family owns the C&A company, an international chain of clothing stores, and its success has led them to become the richest family in the Netherlands.

The company was founded by brothers Clemens and August Brenninkmeijer in 1841 in the Netherlands as a textile company, taking its name from their initials.

Ida was asked to be an aid to two mental weak brothers of C & A president Wolfgang Brenninkmeijer. The head of the C&A Company and his mother Gertrud became firm believers after Ida talked about her apparitions.

When Ida gave exact details about how Mary had looked like, Gertrud Brenninkmeijer want to see it too. So she brought Ida in 1951 to the German artist Heinrich Repke in Wiedenbrück.

Ida: "We went there on the day that the Netherlands was met by a 10 minutes lasting earthquake."

That was on March 14, 1951.

According the descriptions of Ida he tried to paint the 'Lady' standing on the globe.

Ida was not content. She had seen another Lady, younger, and certain not glued to that cross that Repke painted. Also the scarf on her head was quite different. This was the kind of scarf that Judy Garland was wearing, that year making an European tour,. Unlike as what had Ida's Lady on her head: "You could hardly see her hair".

The radio was playing Les Paul & Mary Ford's The World Is Waiting For The Sunshine, followed by the news that the British Witchcraft Act was to be repealed with the enactment of the Fraudulent Mediums Act 1951.

On Friday July 20 is King Abdullah I of Jordan is assassinated near the Dome of the Rock in Jerusalem.

The painting was first placed in the private Chapel of the Brenninkmeijer-estate Haus Langebrück in Mettingen, Germany.

After an imprimatur was obtained from C.N. Meysing (Wassenaar 2-6-1951 Censor a.b. dep) and Dr. F.A. Schweigman O.P. (Neomagi 1-5-1951 Libr. Censor) the image of the Lady of all Peoples , was photographed and printed with the Amsterdam Blessing on the other side.

The bishop of Haarlem, Monsignore Huibers, consulted Professor of Theology Klaas Steur about the theological substance.

About the juridical aspects he asked the judgment of the official C. van Tricht, who reminded the bishop, "that the Church Law warns against the introduction of new devotions, which at times are ridiculous and often useless imitations or even deformations of other acknowledged devotions, which to the non-Catholics give rise to fierce and sometimes even justified opposition".

In February 1955 the first edition of the Messages of Our Lady, known as the *Blue Booklet* was published.

de
Boodschappen
van de
Vrouwe van
alle Volkeren

And after quite a lot of effort it was finally achieved to have the painting of Heinrich Repke placed in a chapel of the Amsterdam Thomas of Aquino-church at the Rijnstraat.

It was in this church that Ida heard the voice of Our Lady during the Eucharistic Adoration, May 31 1955.

Ida: "There were two Volendam women who sat next to me on the knees. Dear god, I know so well ... [laughs] Well, these were there to pray, apparently, when I heard Her voice calling me to the Chapel."

As it was before the final blessing, Ida first tries to ignore it, but the Lady does not stop calling her, so…

Ida: "I went to the chapel and the light followed me. It seemed all light to me, and the crowd all went sideways. They thought of course, that I had become sick or so.

At the beginning, she spoke a few words. Just as a dictation, and said: *Say after me*."

Ida had quite a conversation. Only after the Lady was gone, she realized that she was standing in a crowd: "I was shocked. All those people around me. It was terrible. Because it was always in silence, and nobody beside my family knew about the apparitions for all those years. I would not talk about it with strangers. Well, you know, they would ridicule you and believe that you are crazy."

Soon the priest came who said, *Ida, come with me inside*. Well, the people all wait in front of the church. I left in a taxi from the presbytery at the back of the church in another street."

But after that May 31 1955, reporters and journalists were actually hunting her.

Ida: "Photographers were hiding in the porches around the Thomaschurch. When I noticed it the first time I told my sister: Oh mind you, But she said: You see shadows."

But the next day, her picture was in the papers at the newsstands.

Ida: "I got them down here in the archives. My goodness, it scared me to death.

And then my friends and acquaintances came who said: *Gosh, what do we read, Ida. you've never told us.*"

In order to calm down the commotion around the apparitions, the painting was removed and put up in the parish hall.

Three times a Lady: left the original Heinrich Repke painting, that was made in 1951 in Wiedenbrück, now Rheda-Wiedenbrück in North Rhine-Westphalia, Germany.

When the question around the apparitions began to stir up agitation, bishop Huibers received Ida several times.

On his request she was subjected to intense examinations several times by Professor Carp in Leiden. In his provisional judgment he saw no cause to search for a supernatural explanation.

But the bishop did not want to solely rely on this judgment. So he asked G. van de Burg, dean of Amsterdam, H. van Deursen, president of Warmond, and J. van der Gaag and L. Willebrands, professors of Warmond, to take part in a commission. Also psychologist Mrs. Dr. Perquin, was asked to take part as adviser.

The examination was carried out on the basis of what was described in the 'Blue Booklet'.

Ida: "That committee was against it right from the beginning, so you already have a disadvantage, of course. You will understand how that was addressed. But please, do not say that I have spoken with you. That would give a lot of damage again, then they go back on their rear legs. One of those men is still alive. You've probably seen him on television. Yes, he was the right hand of the bishop and turned against him...".

Ida herself was never invited. Only Dr. Perquin performed several tests on her.

At the conference of June 20, 1955 the members of the commission formulated: "We believe that nobody has bad intentions. Therefore we declare all these revelations, whatsoever, to be of a purely natural origin."

The commission advised the bishop to have the seer psychologically tested once again. Doctor J. de Smet in Heiloo supported the opinion of the members of the commission that the revelations of Our Lady are not of supernatural origin.

The commission believed that apparitions are in fact creatures created by the mind. Our Lady becomes real and out of control, growing in power and boldness, until she goes away.

This theory is given little weight, as there is no convincing scientific evidence that psychokinesis exists, and the consensus view is that Mariology is pseudoscience.

Afterwards it was argued that the commission did not act correctly by not seeing the seer herself.

But with all the documents and pressure produced, the bishop felt obligated to officially disapprove the case 'Amsterdam'. For the '*sake of the integrity of the Church*' he had to declare on 7 May 1956 that "*the commission charged with the examination, concerning the content of the messages themselves and the circumstances, under which the events took place, could not find anything that can not be explained in a fully natural way.*"

The definitive judgment concerning this matter has to be left to the Church. What people wanted to do privately, the bishop did not elaborate.

But the fame of Lady of all Peoples spread abroad. H. Fiechter propagated the devotion in Switzerland

and W. Spanner in Bavaria. Spanner also informed the mission-countries, with the result that everywhere was heard about Our Lady of Amsterdam.

The case 'Amsterdam' had become an issue of the World church. The bishop of Haarlem asked the Holy Office for further instructions.

Joseph cardinal Pizzardo of the Congregation answered and said in his letter that the bishop of Haarlem had acted "very wisely and prudently."

Pizzardo concluded that writings and brochures concerning this case could not get the approval of the Church.

This was a new blow to Ida and all those all over the world, who steadfastly believed in the apparitions.

One year later, on the night of February 18, 1958, Ida woke up at three o'clock. A day earlier Pope Pius XII had declared Saint Clare the patron saint of television.

In Ida's own words:

"I heard someone call me. I saw the light again and heard the voice of the Lady saying: Here I am again... I shall make an announcement that you may not tell anyone about, including the Sacrista (Van Lierde) and your spiritual director. When it has happened, you may tell them that the Lady told it to you at this time.

This Holy Father, Pope Pius XII, will be taken up among Us at the beginning of October of this year.'

First thing in the morning, Ash Wednesday, Ida calls Father Frehe to tell him that the Lady has given her a message, but that she may tell no one about it.

Fr. Frehe: "You have to promise me to write down everything immediately, and to bring it straight to me today.

Otherwise it is worthless.

Think about it.

I don't care whether you seal the letter; it's only important that I receive it today, and preferably as soon as possible."

Ida types the Lady's words, keeps a copy and takes the sealed original to Frehe.

September 27 a typhoon named Ida kills at least 1,269 in Honshū, Japan.

October 9 Pius XII dies.

Ida immediately hurries to Father Frehe to ask for the sealed envelope.

He sends the sealed original that same day to the diocese. The bishop then sent all documents to Rome, indicating in an enclosed letter, that he felt to have found something significant.

Ida writes in a letter to her bishop, Mgr.. Huibers, on November 24, 1958, "On the morning of October 9, while sitting before the radio, I then heard that the Holy Father had died. After that I said, 'Thanks be to God.' I know, of course, that this was not nice of me, but he will forgive me, for he knows that I was saying it to the Lady, for not abandoning us, and for not discrediting her concerns ..."

Later in private Bishop Huibers would admit that from this moment on, he believed in the Apparitions.

His Exc. Most Reverend Jan Huibers, Bishop of Haarlem/Amsterdam.

Ida: "Yes he told me he was very happy that Our Lady appeared in his diocese.

But he was put under high pressure by fanatics who said that apparitions were out of time, and that the Bishop had to confirm the decision with consent of Pizzardo."

Pope John XXIII succeeds Pius XII on October 28 1958 as the 261st pope.

And as the Lady showed Ida in a vision: the new pope announces on January 25 1959 that a Second Vatican Council will be convened in Rome.

It opened under John XXIII on October 11, 1962 and closed under Paul VI on December 8, 1965.

The Church that Mary want to be build.

Ida: "I heard that in India a large painting is made of the Lady, for the church the lady asked to be built here in Amsterdam. But it was such a typical church the Lady showed me. [Laughs] It was so crazy, what I saw it, I thought, well that is not a Catholic church. That would have towers and everything, but this one had domes, yes. Three cupolas. Very strange. It was a kind of ... I thought…"

That is was a mosque?

"Yes, something like that".

Perhaps was that the intention?

Ida: "No, no"!

They must have a very thick file on you, in the diocese of Haarlem. There was an other inquiry.

Ida: "Oh, well, that was a nice commission, I can tell you all about. [laughs scamper] I could not talk about the appearances, but how I was at school, how I had been, what I had done. And I had that sign. I thought: this is the good way, I was pleased with that investigation, believing that the truth always prevail.

But Kuiper said: 'Be not so happy, because it will be the same, that the case will be prohibited again.

Well, no wonder. I guess that they have written a very bad report on it.

In 1959 Louis Knuvelder (1907-1982) published, without Imprimatur, his 'Maria en de verschijningen te Amsterdam' ('Mary and the apparitions of Amsterdam'). Which book was after consultation with the Holy Office put on the Index of prohibited books.

When in 1960 a new bishop, Mgr. J. Van Dodewaard came to Haarlem, he was requested, a.o. by author Louis Knuvelder, to reopen the investigation. The bishop replied that he would orientate himself. But as long as no new apparitions would emerge, it was imprudent to open up a new investigation.

In the circles of the proponents one presumed that the bishop would change his mind when the Holy Office would give green light for a new investigation. To achieve this, a petition of four professors of Theology was sent to the Holy See, asking for a new investigation. The case reached the Holy Office and after consulting with the bishop of Haarlem it was concluded, that there was no reason to reopen the case of the 'Lady'. The Holy Office explained literally: (Prot. N.511/53)

After careful consultation the Holy Office has decided, that the case is definitely clear and that one should retract from the subject: the messages are false and remain forbidden for publication.

Shortly after the renewed dismissal the Congregation of the Holy Office communicated:

'They had good intentions and they want to defend the honor of Mary. We do however mean, that the case now is closed for good and that further investigations are no longer necessary.

This second attempt, to get the World church interested in 'Amsterdam' fell in the midst of the Council and many bishops asked for an explanation.

The bishop of Haarlem had a unbiased note drawn up, translated into Latin, which he distributed among the council fathers, hoping that the case of the 'Lady' would be shelved altogether.

However, the bishop was wrong. Enthusiasts gathered monthly in Amsterdam and recruited supporters in Germany and France. They tried through a backdoor to get Church-approval.

The renowned book of Knuvelder, reprinted in 1966, was offered for an Imprimatur to a mission-bishop of Doume (Cameroon), who had shown much interest. When he declared, that he was not authorized to give the Imprimatur, the book was presented to the bishop of Den Bosch, who, very correctly, referred to the decisions, made about the case at the bishops conference.

When in 1966 Mgr. Zwartkruis came as the new bishop to Haarlem the supporters got new hope. The bishop refuted their argument, that the preceding investigations had been incomplete because one had neglected to interrogate the most important persons. He pointed out, that it was the seer's own wish, to be kept out of the interrogations. But this was not accepted just like that.

Because bishop Zwartkruis wished to get the confusion around this case once and for all out of the world, he decided in 1972 to reassess the case, whereby he let the supporters know, that they should not have too high expectations.

SACRA CONGREGATIO
PRO DOCTRINA FIDEI

Roma, le 24 mai 1972

Prot. N. 511/53

Excellence,

Dans votre lettre du début d'avril de cette année vous informez cette Congrégation des conclusions auxquelles est arrivée la Commission spéciale, établie par Votre Excellence, pour étudier encore une fois le cas des prétendues apparitions et révélations d'Amsterdam, et vous vous proposez de rétracter les prohibitions relatives à la diffusion de la dévotion de la "Vrouwe van alle volkeren".

Ce Dicastère comprend bien votre sollicitude pastorale qui voudrait améliorer à moyen d'une rétractation un climat de tension, mais il estime que cette rétractation entraînerait des effets déplorables. Vu que l'image de la "Vrouwe van alle volkeren" ainsi que les prières accompagnantes accusent une relation très étroite avec les révélations prétendues, une levée des prohibitions ne manquerait pas à être interprétée comme un "nihil obstat" aux révélations, voire, comme une approbation tacite. Si maintenant, malgré les prohibitions, on se trouve devant une campagne vigoureusement menée, on se demande ce que les promoteurs feraient quand les prohibitions auraient été levées.

D'ailleurs la position initiale prise par votre prédécesseur S.E.Mgr. J.P.Huibers a été confirmée à plusieurs reprises par ce Dicastère dans les termes les plus clairs.

En vu de cela cette Congrégation retient que les prohibitions relatives à la diffusion du message et au culte publique doivent être maintenues.

Veuillez agréer, Excellence, l'expression de mes sentiments religieux et dévoués.

Fran. Card. Seper, Préf.

A Son Excellence
Mgr. Th. ZWARTKRUIS
Evêque de Haarlem - Hollande

Letter of May, 24, 1972 concerning the Amsterdam Apparitions by Cardinal Seper, head of the Sacra Congregatio pro Doctrina Fidei.

A commission of nine members under the chairmanship of vicar H. Kuipers started a third investigation. The findings were presented to the Holy Office. On May 24, 1972 Cardinal Seper, head of the Congregation, endorsed one of the conclusions, namely that also now no reason had been found to acknowledge a supernatural origin of the messages, while the other conclusion, to lift the prohibition orders regarding the adoration of the 'Lady', because of pastoral considerations and offered as an advice, was turned down by Seper, notwithstanding the fact that some people wanted to indulge deeper into the subject.

The members of the committee together with bishop Zwartkruis, held a press conference during and issued a communiqué in which they repeated that they could not find a supernatural origin in the events of Amsterdam, ant that Rome supported this view. Although this view was based on the finding of the Commission Kuipers.

Whenever the case came into discussion again, the diocese confined itself to the above mentioned press communiqué, which was translated into several languages.

During her lifetime it was a coming and going of all kind of people. The simple Ida with her two year Advanced Education had adherents in the highest circles. With her genuine simplicity Ida stole the hearts of nobles as Franz Graf von Magnis and mgr. Van Lierde, personal sexton of the pope. She moved with ease in the to outsiders hermetically sealed Brenninkmeijer family.

Beside reporters and the representatives of the Roman Catholic Church, all sorts of controversial figures sought contact. Hoped to pick a grain of the apparitions. All what was Underground Catholic made its way to the southern part of Amsterdam.

In 1962 the sister of Ida received a phone call with the announcement that The Pope would come along to the Peerdeman house. Without answering she smashed the horn on the devise. But a little later the phone rang again.

It was Fr. Frehe. He told that a devotee to the Amsterdam apparitions had asked if he could see Ida with a French priest that was dying to see her.

Alright, a priest Ida never refused. It turned out that the priest was the Frenchman Michel Colin (1905-1974). Ordained a priest in 1935, but reduced to the lay state in 1951.

The Peerdeman-sisters would never receive the man if they had known that Pope Pius XII had declared him a *vitandus* (one who should be avoided).

That was because Michel Colin claimed to be "crowned Pope by the Archangels". That happened on October 7, 1950 in the French village of Clémery. Where Colin build his Counter Vatican out of some stables, telling the world that he was pope Clement XV, and that the Pope of Rome was a fake.

Ida: "I met him just once in my house, because he found it necessary to come to me. He came in a brand new black cassock, with all buttons and a new sash too. So he was completely in the new and started to grumble at Rome. That they were so mean, and they had him ... I said to him that it is good, that Rome is very strict.

The person who came with him said to me: 'Well, how can you say this, you've seen Mary, how can you say that they have to be strict'? I answered: 'Yes, they should be strict, and they must also be tough on me.'

I gave him quite the truth, and he was furious.

The man that had come with him said 'The pope will be kicked out the Vatican, and here is the new Pope.'

Well, one of my sisters gave a scream of laughter and asked: 'Oh man, aren't you out of your mind?'

The 'pope' got a red head, got up and he went to the wardrobe to take his hat and was gone.

My sister opened all the windows and sprinkled the place where he had been with holy water!

Yes, we have experienced such crazy things, you know. Oh dear."

Ida: "When he was gone, I immediately called that gentleman that brought this 'pope' to our place to tell him that he should watch out for that man. He said: 'Oh, we have heaven in our house'. He even had said a mass here.'

Antipope Clement XV (Michel Colin 1905-1974) on his way to Ida Peerdeman.

I said: 'Oh yeah? Well, I've had a hell in my house when this man was here. But you hear me, if you continue with this Clement XV thing, you are no longer welcome in the Amsterdam Uiterwaarden-straat 408 3rd floor. That was it."

Clement XV had been brought up by the police later, after he walked here in Amsterdam with a papal white robe."

Who was that man that brought that guy to you?

Ida: "There were a couple, nice people, good friends, who came often to visit us in the evening. The two had a bunch of children they did not see no more."

For a long time Ida did not see the couple. The man that was with the 'pope' had suddenly kidnapped Ida's apparitions and founded a chapel for the 'Glorious Lady of all Nations' on the Amsterdam Amstelveenseweg.

Ida: "He had painted an awful ugly copy after our prayer card. That stood in the window of their chapel. There were also sisters, for their supposed veneration of the Lady of all Nations, which I believe were all in blue, with a blue scarf and so on."

But it was child's play compared what Ida was awaiting when the Canadian prophetess Marie-Paule Giguère kidnapped her apparition.

September 1967 Marie-Paule Giguère saw in the Catholic bookstore of Quebec City a book about the Amsterdam Apparition. She thumbed through the book, put it back and left the store.

A few days later she received this book by mail from lady friend Rose Dessureault. She saw this as a direct divine intervention from heaven. And had to re-read this writing by Raoul Auclair five times.

Soon the shrine in her hometown Etchemin was transformed into a sanctuary for the Lady of all Nations. Where the members of her group, hailed from Canada and the United States, gathered on Saint Augustine-day for an annual day of prayer.

On August 28, 1971 Marie-Paule founded at this Shrine her Communauté de la Dame de tous les Peuples (Community of the Lady of all Peoples). The members all dressed in white, like the Amsterdam apparition. Marie-Paule was the inspiring force behind a fast growing international Marian Group, devoted to the Lady of all Nations.

After the death of the Dominican Frehe, that held the reins of Ida tightly where necessary, the more theological Dr. G.Th.H. Liesting became Ida's spiritual mainstay. For whom the apparition where an interesting theological case. As evidenced by his introduction to the messages of the Lady of All Nations under the title It will come with time, published in 1970.

Liesting his book is released at a time a Marian Apparition was considered the most backward manifestation of the Catholic church in modern times. Many tapped their forehead, and not as the beginning of the cross sign.

After the death of Liesting it was Father Jan Kerssemakers sss who became in 1971 the permanent priest in the chapel, and confessor of Ida Peerdeman.

He is 18 years younger as Ida.

Kerssemakers became Ida's support, shelter and watchdog. Straightforward and to the point he could brute snub people off if something did not please him. And he turned mad if a question was asked he did not want to hear.

Like one day Ida was asked if the priests in her vision of the Great Church to be built *were just ordinary priests*. Kerssemakers was nicked "the doorman of the Lady."

March 20, 1973 Marie-Paule Giguère, her mother Laura Bégin, ladyfriend Rose Dessureault and Father Philippe Roy headed for Amsterdam

Ida: "This Marie-Paule was introduced to me through the sacristan of the Pope himself, Mgr. Van Lierde.

In volume VIII of Life of Love the Canadian writes:

"At eleven o'clock, we meet with the seeress, Miss Ida Peerdeman, and her director Father Kerssemakers. We discuss the book, 'The Lady of All Peoples', and we furnish the explanations that are needed. Miss Ida wrote this book without understanding the meaning and significance of what it contains."

The next year, September 1974, the Communauté de la Dame de tous les Peuples set out on a first Grand Pilgrimage to Amsterdam. With no less than 332 all white "knights".

Ida: "Marie-Paule Giguère had rented the Krijtberg (litt.: Chalkmountain, nick for a Jesuit church in Amsterdam) for an evening prayer service and called me if I could come. We went to see what was going on that night in the church. She sat there on the altar, sang some songs and all the people of her club had to kneel for her, and give her a kiss."

All over Europe Marie-Paule and her Army make promotion for the Amsterdam Apparitions.

She managed that images of the Lady of all Nations was carried at the head of processions in Lourdes, surrounded by the Swiss Guard. Also in Fatima, Paris, Lisieux and Assisi Her flags and banners are waved. Highlight of the trip is when the Amsterdam Madonna is placed next to the altar during a solemn ceremony held at Saint Peter's Basilica in Rome.

That moment Giguère is devout kneeling down for the effigy, stating with tears in her eyes that "The Mother of All Nations is home at last!"

In October 1974, the Chairman of the Amsterdam Lady of all Peoples Foundation Herman Brouwer is complaining about the visit of Marie-Paule to Ida:

Very opinionated she told Ida how she had to interpret the message of the Lady. It seems that she is publishing a book with her explanation of the messages of the Lady, well-mixed with her own messages. May the Lord help us!

Two months later, December 3, 1974, Brouwer writes to the Vicar General of His Holiness in Rome Mgr. Petrus Canisius J. van Lierde about *a certain Mrs. M. Paule from Canada*, sending letters to Ida Peerdeman, telling her *how she should act and how she had to understand the messages*. Fortunately Ida disregard these confusing letters, but Ida is not very happy with her writing.

Anyhow, the 'Army of Mary' of Marie-Paule Giguère was officially recognized by canonical Decree by the Archbishop of Quebec on March 10, 1975.

Despite the objections, Giguère led her Knights *in a crusade of prayer and penance* for four years in a row to Amsterdam.

On Thursday, September 22, 1977 a new contingent left Montreal for the Netherlands. Another group would join the next day, bringing the total number of pilgrims to three hundred and fifty.

The sojourn with Ida and her director Father Kerssemakers was "at four o'clock in the afternoon" September 23, 1977, as Marie-Paule recounted in volume XV of Life of Love.

After this visit Giguère and her Knights continued their penance crusade into Europe and the Holy Land.

In Rome the White Knights stayed at the Villa Pamphili Hotel. During the afternoon of October 4, fire broke out at the hotel.

The firemen arrived quickly, putting up a latter to the roof from which black smoke was billowing, as it was from certain windows. Most of the Knights headed outside, while a few stood on their balconies. Others still trying to locate the exits.

Once they were reassured that no one had been forgotten inside the building, under the enquiring glances of other people present the White Knights began singing the *Magnificat*.

According to Marie-Paule Giguère: *And suddenly... the smoke began to progressively dissipate and the firemen left without having even used their equipment... Then everything became quiet once again.*

The pilgrims hastened to return to their rooms where they had the surprise of *finding their white clothing completely untouched, even though the furniture and the floors were covered with black soot.*

This *miracle* was attributed to the Lady of all Nations.

The last leg of this trip led the White Army to Fatima where the 60th anniversary of the Virgin's apparitions to the children Lucia, Jacinta and Francesco was celebrated.

In May 1979 Marie-Paule published the first of fourteen volumes of her autobiography Life of Love. The other thirteen French volumes would be published in the next year. She suggest a close relationship between her spirituality and the apparitions of Mary in Amsterdam.

Archbishop Marc Ouellet of Quebec asked in 2004 the Bishop of Haarlem-Amsterdam about it, but beside the visits made in the 70s there was never a connection established between the devotion to the Lady of all Peoples and the Community of the Lady of all Peoples of Marie-Paule Giguère.

Ida realized that the Canadian had kidnapped her apparition when Madame Giguère declared that she herself was the incarnation of Ida's Lady of all Peoples.

According Marie-Paule Giguère, it was Ida Peerdeman that wrote a letter to Vatican's Mgr. Van Lierde about her:

Who is this woman?

Is she a second Catharine of Sienna?

A second Jeanne d'Arc?

Does our Church-History know anyone similar?

We believe that she is exceptional.

I even would go so far as to proclaim her to be, in an exceptional way, the Incarnation of the Holy Virgin Mary, the Co-Redemptrix, the Mediatrix and the Advocate: The Lady of all Nations."

Short before her death Ida assured me that she had *never* wrote such a letter. In the archives of the

Foundation of the Lady of all Peoples, and the diocese is no document to find that supports the allegations of Mrs. Giguère, or even refers to.

As this Canadian Army of Mary movement mixes the cult of the Lady of all Peoples with the ideas of Marie-Paule it discredited the entire devotion.

Some of the predictions and claims of Madame Giguère in her books:

Jesus appears to Marie-Paule, and told her: Whoever kisses your photo will be instantaneously cured. (book 8, p.39)

Mgr. Van Lierde is offered the papacy, which he "humbly" accepts. (book 13 p. 46). Once Pope he will canonize Marie-Paule Giguère as the first person to be declared Saint during lifetime (book I p.199).

The best had to come: On September 11, 1975 she even united herself and Ida Peerdeman in a 'mystical marriage' with Monsignore Van Lierde.

Ida was not aware that she was involved in this 'mystical marriage'.

It ended, of course, in a 'divorce', when Mgr. Van Lierde realized that he was a kind of mystical Pasha with a harem of two woman.

At the end Marie-Paule and her Army were excommunicated for heretical teachings and beliefs by the Roman Congregation for the Doctrine of the Faith.

In a press release September 2007 the diocese of Haarlem-Amsterdam distancing itself from the Canadian Cult.

But still there is a huge statue of the Amsterdam Madonna on the roof of the building of the International Headquarters of Marie-Paule Giguère's Community of the Lady of all Nations in Canada.

Ida's watchdog Jan Kerssemakers sss, died at the age of 58 in 1981, while saying Mass in the Chapel.

Ida and her sisters are shocked by his unexpected and early death.

There is an attempt to have the priest to be buried in the garden of the Diepenbrockstraat.

The assumption was that the former Brenninkmeijer villa had become a real monastery, with the right to maintain a cemetery.

That failed.

So Father Kerssemakers is buried at the Roman Catholic cemetery Buitenveldert. The place where also Gertrude and Wolfgang Brenninkmeijer found their final resting place.

The grave of Father Kerssemakers is decorated with a very expensive bronze image of the Lady of all Peoples.

Later there is another entombment on the St. Barbara Cemetery, where the sisters Peerdeman had bought a family tomb.

Also the bronze statue of Our Lady is moved to there.

Ida talked two extended nights with me. At that time she was waiting for over 50 years in vain that the Church would recognize her apparitions.

But there was no sign that the Church would do so.

The contrary. In 1956 the local bishop felt obliged to point out that the 'public devotion' of Mary as the 'Lady of all Peoples' could not yet be permitted. The Holy Office, as published in L'Osservatore Romano of 14-15 June 1974 also found no reason to acknowledge the supernatural origin of her messages.

And on April 26, 1987 Joseph cardinal Ratzinger confirmed explicitly the validity of that declaration.

But Ida was sure: *Don't worry, it will be recognized!*

According to the doctrine of the Catholic Church, an authentic apparition is believed not to be a subjective experience, but a real and objective intervention of divine power.

A Marian apparition, if deemed genuine by Church authority, is treated as private revelation that may emphasize some facet of the received public revelation for a specific purpose. The era of public revelation ended with the death of the last living Apostle. So Mary can never add anything new to the deposit of faith.

In the 2003, the Vatican yearbook revealed that between 1905 and 1995 there were 295 reported apparitions, only 11 of which were recognized as genuine.

The church states that cures and other miraculous events are not the purpose of Marian apparitions, but exist primarily to validate and draw attention to the message.

Apparitions of Mary are held to be evidence of her continuing active presence in the life of the church, through which she "cares for the brethren of her son who still journey on earth."

The Church will confirm an apparition as worthy of belief, but belief is never required by divine faith.

While Marian apparitions may at times seem like fanciful tales, factual analysis indicates that the effect of apparitions on the Roman Catholic Church has been significant. Marian apparitions are responsible for tens of millions of Marian pilgrimages per year.

About 10 million pilgrims visit Our Lady of Guadalupe each year, where each mass can accommodate up to 40,000 people. And 5 million pilgrims visit Lourdes every year and within France only Paris has more hotels than Lourdes. Thus each decade, just Lourdes and Guadalupe amount to over one hundred million Catholic pilgrimages, based on Marian apparitions to two people on two remote hilltops.

The Sanctuary of Our Lady of Fatima also attracts a large number of Roman Catholics, and every year pilgrims fill the country road that leads to the shrine with crowds that approach one million on May 13 and October 13, the significant dates of Fatima apparitions.

Marian apparitions have affected the Catholic Church with the spread of Marian devotions such as the rosary and the construction of some of the largest churches ever.

Marian apparitions have also influenced the direction of Roman Catholic Mariology, as illustrated by the ex cathedra exercise of Papal infallibility on the dogma of Immaculate Conception. This also illustrated that unlike most Roman Catholic theology which originates from the upper levels of the Church, Mariology has quite often been driven from the ground up by the tens of millions of Catholics with a special devotion to the Blessed Virgin.

But it has been claimed that apparitions also were experienced by a number of popes, including Pope Leo XIII in 1884, Pope Pius XII at various stages during his papacy, and Pope John Paul II in 1981, while he recovered from an assassination attempt which occurred on May 13, the anniversary of the Fatima apparition.

As Marian apparitions create strong emotions among large numbers of Roman Catholics, they lead to *sensus fidelium*. This strong response among Catholics in turn influences the higher levels of the Roman Catholic hierarchy as *sensus fidei* gains strength.

The first known Marian apparition took place, according tradition, in the year 39 AD, when the Virgin Mary appeared to Saint James the Great, in Zaragoza, Spain. The vision is now called Our Lady of the Pillar and is the only reported Marian apparition before her Assumption.

Possibly the best-known apparition sites are Lourdes and Fatima, with its hundreds of millions of Marian pilgrimages.

The so-called Three Secrets of Fatima received a great deal of attention in the Catholic and secular press.

Next to Beatrix Park in Amsterdam in the Netherlands, is the residence build for Gertrud, the mother of Wolf Brenninkmeijer, president of C&A, international chain of clothing stores.

The garage of this unassuming building, houses the chapel that draws thousands of pilgrims who come to pray before the miraculous painting representing Mary as "Lady of All Peoples".

The tableau is painted according the apparition of the Blessed Virgin as she appeared in Amsterdam and Germany on numerous occasions between 1945 and 1959. In this little chapel the Lady of All Peoples is doing her miracles from behind state-of-the-art bullet proof glass.

Ida Peerdeman.

Ida's life was filled with moral sufferings. It was very difficult for her to share her experiences, in part because of adversaries and refusals, and also in part because of her own concern to always transmit everything as faithfully as possible. For years, she only wished to disappear, to remain unknown, absolutely not wanting a role in the forefront. How often did she not repeat: *"It is not I; I am merely an instrument; dashing out Our Lady's messages."*

The interest of the World-church for the question of the 'Lady of all Peoples' never faded away.

Monsignore Hendrik Joseph Alois Bomers, C.M succeeded as the bishop of Haarlem. To some, this man was saintly. On April 26, 1987 Joseph cardinal Ratzinger confirmed the declaration of May 1974 and declared that the 'declaration' of the Congregation dated May 25 1974 (in accordance to L'Osservatore Romano of 14-15 June 1974), concerning the so-called apparitions of Amsterdam has not been revoked or modified and therefore remains completely in force.

Despite this affirmation of cardinal Ratzinger, Father Peter Klos sss, starts to publish a bulletin in the Dutch language, 'Queen of the Prophets', in which he deals, besides 'Amsterdam', with mystical phenomena.

Ida Peerdeman disapproved this, especially when he tried to propagate 'Medjugorje' in the chapel in Amsterdam.

Ida was waiting in Vain that the Church would recognize her Apparitions.

I told her that I've heard that Rome will consider the case again.

Ida: "Yes, yes. That's right. In Rome there is no problem. It's only here, monsignor Bomers still has difficulty with his surroundings, right. They don't want it. They say: 'Apparitions are no longer an issue in this time, and so on...

Has monsignor Bomers been with you?

Ida pauses: ... I can ... that I may not answer.

Is it all so difficult, is it all so ... how should you say... there are two parties in the church, the conservative and the modernists. So those fight against each other.

The modernists are against apparitions. And the Church must be very careful. As the Church should also be careful with me, I always used to say.

The case of Our Lady is really fifty years sustained by the people in the whole world. I mean, millions of prayer cards, translated into more than 80 languages, have already been spread throughout the whole world and images of the Lady of all Peoples have been placed in many churches and chapels for veneration. the people continue to order the messages and prayer cards. I get requests to send prayers and books to the Philippines, Australia, America, France, England, you name it. All over the world images of the Lady of all Peoples have been placed in churches and chapels for veneration.

A bishop from Rome said to me,: Ida, it has been fifty years, and after fifty years we can see that everything that Our Lady predicted, is released. We live at the moment in the middle of her messages. And that is true.

It was all given in short phrases. What I saw there with it, that was never written down. Which I should not. It had to be purely the words of Mary and not what I saw there. But I have seen what happens now, I have seen those diseases like AIDS. Yes, previously you knew nothing about AIDS, so then I thought it was cholera. But now you see it on television, so I wake up and realize what it was the Lady showed me.

NOTIFICATION

for the catholic faithful of the diocese of Haarlem

We, the Bishop and Auxiliary Bishop of Haarlem have, for a long time and in increasing numbers, received requests both from home and abroad. These requests are for us to provide clarification regarding the status of the apparitions of Mary as 'THE LADY OF ALL NATIONS', in Amsterdam, during the years 1945-1959.

After ample consideration and consultation of official authorities, we have decided to adopt the following policy in order to provide the required pastoral clarity:

Distinction must be made between the apparitions/messages on the one hand and the Marian title 'The Lady of All Nations', on the other hand.

At the moment the Church cannot make a pronouncement about the supernatural character of the apparitions and the content of the messages. One is free to make a personal judgement according to his or her own conscience.

The prayer 'Lord Jesus Christ.....' which includes the title 'The Lady of All Nations', has since 1951 enjoyed Church approval by Msgr. Huibers, who was Bishop of Haarlem at the time. It is our judgement that there is no objection against the public veneration of The Blessed Virgin Mary under this title.

In an age where races, peoples and cultures are more dependent on each other than ever before - nowhere more so than in Amsterdam - we have confidence in saying that it is exactly this title which throws a clear light on our Lady's Universal Motherhood and her unique role as 'women' in God's plan of Salvation.

Haarlem, May 31, 1996, the feast of The Visitation of Mary.

† Henricus Bomars
Bishop of Haarlem

† Joseph Punt
Auxiliary

Nieuwe Gracht 80 - Postbox 1053, 2001 BB Haarlem
Tel. 023-5319450 - Fax 023- 5341405 - Postbank 4 3509

Ida had been promised by the Lady that she would not die before seeing the public veneration of the Lady of all Peoples.

The Lady was true to Her word. On May 31, 1996 Bishop Hendrik Bomers, C.M. of Haarlem, in collaboration with his auxiliary Bishop Punt, authorized the public devotion of the Lady of All Peoples.

"At the moment the Church cannot make a pronouncement about the supernatural character of the apparitions and the content of the messages. One is free, to make a personal judgment according to his or her own conscience".

Ida had lived to see it.

"Now I can die", Ida had said when she was informed of this news. She had not flinched. She did not waver. She did not fail. Ida died the following June 17, at the age of ninety.

His Excellency Bishop Bomers presided over her Requiem Mass held in the garage-chapel and the funeral on the Amsterdam St Barbara cemetery.

On August 22, 1996 abbot Nicolaas de Wolff osb, the former boss of the abbey Sint-Benedictusberg in Vaals, the Netherlands, crowned the painting of the 'Lady of all Peoples' in the chapel in Amsterdam. In the meantime he has moved from the Abbey of Vaals to the Priory Gräfinthal in Mandelbachthal, Germany.

For the Slovakian bishop Paul Maria Hnilica s.j., titular bishop of Rusado, and his helper, Austrian Father Paul Maria Sigl (Paul Gebhart), 'Amsterdam' is the very thing.

Since the bishop now allows the public veneration they both together organize grandiose international prayer days in honor of the 'Lady of all Peoples' in the RAI-Halls in Amsterdam, and well for the first time in May 1997 with no less than 12.000 visitors.

During this day bishop Hnilica laid the connections between Fatima and the messages of 'Amsterdam'. Bishop Hnilica claimed that the messages of 'Amsterdam' contained the so-called 'Third Secret of Fatima'.

On June 20, 1997 bishop Bomers declared: "for the diocese of Haarlem I have declared that there is no objection against the public veneration of the Blessed Virgin Mary under the title *Lady of all Peoples*. I will only be happy, if this devotion finds acceptance elsewhere too, provided the local ordinary does agree."

Assistant bishop Punt declares on October 4, 1997, that he is "pleased to support the veneration of Mary under the title *Lady of all Peoples* and furthermore and that he "is pleased to encourage the *Action of the Lady of all Peoples*, the goal of which is the spreading of her image and prayer throughout the world."

During the second International Prayer Day in 1998 a greeting of the prioress of the convent of the only still living Fatima-seer, sister Lucia, was read to the audience, which made great impression.

That day Bomers declared:

'Based on the fruits that more and more become noticeable, I have together with my assistant bishop decided, to set up a commission, in order to gather and study all testimonies concerning the events of the 'Lady and Mother of all nations'.

Bishop Bomers suddenly died on September 12, 1998, the apostolic administrator Punt took over.

After the third Prayer day in 1999 Punt declares, that 'the commission of investigation around the events of the 'Lady of all Peoples' in Amsterdam has not yet been established, though they approached some people in the meantime".

During the third International Prayer Day in 1999 a 'bridge was built' between Fatima and 'Amsterdam'. Members of the Blue Army of Austria brought with them two big wooden statues of the Lady of Amsterdam, which apostolic administrator Punt was invited to crown with a crown which was blessed by the Pope.

In 2001 Monsignore Hnilica and Father Sigl organized 'national' prayer days in Ireland, Austria, Switzerland, England, Germany and Slovakia. There would be preparations for prayer days also in America, the Philippines and India. Also in the Netherlands a national prayer day was organized, with bishop Hnilica and Father Sigl as speakers.

His Exc. Most Reverend Joseph Marianus Punt,
Bishop of Haarlem/Amsterdam.

On May 31, 2002, Jos Punt, Bishop of Haarlem/Amsterdam, concluded a 45 year period of investigation: the apparitions of Ida Peerdeman are of a supernatural origin.

In Response to Inquiries Concerning the Lady of all Peoples Apparitions he writes:

As Bishop of Haarlem/Amsterdam, I have been requested to make a statement regarding the authenticity of the apparitions of Mary as the Lady of all Peoples in Amsterdam during the years of 1945 -1959.

Many members of the faithful and bishops have emphasized the urgency for clarification. I also have been personally aware that this development of devotion, which has spanned over 50 years, call for this.

As it is known, my predecessor, Mgr.. H. Bomers and myself had previously given permission for public veneration in 1996.

As to the supernatural character of the apparitions and contents of the messages, we did not give our judgment, but declared that "everyone is free to make a judgment for himself or herself according to their conscience."

Having had a generally positive attitude towards authenticity, we decided to await further development and to "discern the spirit" further (cf. 1 Thes 5:19-21).

Over the period of six subsequent years, I observed that the devotion had taken its place in the spiritual life of millions all over the world, and that it possesses the support of many bishops.

Many experiences of conversion and reconciliation, as well as healings and special protection also have been reported to me.

In full recognition of the responsibility of the Holy See, it is primarily the task of the local bishop to speak out in conscience regarding the authenticity of private revelations that take place or have taken place within his diocese.

Therefore I have asked once again for the advice of theologians and psychologists concerning outcomes of previous investigations, and the questions and objections deriving from them.

Their recommendations state that no theological or psychological impediments for a declaration of supernatural authenticity can be found therein. I have also requested the judgment of a number of brother bishops concerning the fruits and development of the devotion, who within their own dioceses have experienced a strong devotion of Mary as the Mother and Lady of all Peoples.

In light and virtue of all these recommendations, testimonies, and developments, and in pondering all this in prayer and theological reflection, I have come to the conclusion that the apparitions of the Lady of all Peoples in Amsterdam consist of a supernatural origin.

Naturally, the influence of the human element still exists. Authentic images and visions are always transmitted to us, in the words of Joseph Cardinal Ratzinger, Prefect of the Congregation of the Doctrine of Faith, "through the filter of our senses, which carry out a work of translation..." and "...are influenced by the potentialities and limitations of the perceiving subject" (Cardinal Ratzinger, Theological Commentary In Preparation for the Release of the Third Part of the Secret of Fatima, L 'Osservatore Romano, June 28, 2000).

Unlike Holy Scripture, private revelations are never binding upon the conscience of the faithful.

They are a help in understanding the signs of the times and to help live more fully the Gospel (cf. Lk 12:56, Catechism of the Catholic Church, n. 67).

And the signs of our times are dramatic. The devotion to the Lady of all Peoples can help us, in my sincere conviction, in guiding us on the right path during the present serious drama of our times, the path to a new and special outpouring of the Holy

Spirit, Who alone can heal the great wounds of our times.

To follow the further development of this devotion and to come to an even deeper insight into its meaning,

I have installed a commission whose task it will be to continue to document all initiatives, experiences, and testimonies stemming from the devotion in order to help insure and preserve a correct ecclesial and theological progress of devotion.

I hope this has provided sufficient information and clarification.

Signed in Haarlem May 31, 2002
Bishop J.M. Punt of Haarlem-Amsterdam.

This decree ends a 45 year period of investigation.

Just like Lourdes or Fatima, also the apparitions of Amsterdam has its antagonists.

Four people, united in a foundation called *Vaak* (Often), refused to accept that the Amsterdam apparitions were official licensed by the only responsible authority to judge in these matters.

It were Pastor Rudo Franken and the laymen Nico Alles, Mark Waterinckx, and Hildegard Alles.

Before the approval their Foundation was aiming to provide information about current appearances and natural phenomena *in the light of decisions of the competent ecclesiastical authority.*

But when asked, the diocese of Roermond refused to give an 'imprimatur' or even a 'nihil obstat' on their quarterly newsletter. As this does not apply to publications on non-approved apparitions.

The Bishop of Roermond wrote: "Until these are recognized either definitively rejected, they remain a point of disagreement, where people could freely discuss, even in the Church".

Notwithstanding ecclesiastic approval in 2002, nor the claim that the Vaak foundation was guided by *decisions of the competent ecclesiastical authority,* they raised hell.

Mark Waterinckx, main contributor of the Vaak-newsletter with a circulation of 2000 copies, left after he was accused by Nico Alles for having *communist sympaties.*

Dr. David Berger, editor-in-chief of the German Newsletter 'Theologisches' was misguided by a set-up of two Amsterdam adversaries: Anton Bongers and Hildegard Alles, resulting in the publication of an article by Mrs. Alles in the German Newsletter.

On the Dutch internet forum *De omstreden Stichting Vaak*, The Dubious Vaak Foundation, there were quite some reactions.

Thom Vandenburg, from Perth, Australia was just one of them. On July the 6th 2005 he wrote: 'Boasting of Mrs. Alles is pure poppycock'.

Vandenburg called it interesting stuff, 'as the Mother of all Nations is here more popular as those apparitions of Lourdes!'

He said that the late Mr. Anton Bongers was 'not well gasp by pretending not to know the difference between Medjugorje and Amsterdam.' Neither was Dr. David Berger 'Kosher, for having the knowledge that Amsterdam is ecclesiastic approved and even Ratzinger showed his assent to Monsignor Punt! Check it out!'

What fronted as a serious study by Mrs. Hildegard Alles in 'Thelogisches' he called 'theological fiddling', 'merely poppycock' and 'Ein lauttönendes Nichts!'

What can best be translated as *a ballyhoo wind*!

And this poppycock was not even her own work, as Norbert Noecker stated on July 9, 2005: "If you could read Dutch, you would see that the article by Mrs. Hildegard Alles was copied from an earlier writing by the self proclaimed Marian scholar Dr. Mark Waterinckx from Flanders."

Others on the Vaak-forum made similar judgements about the 'study' of Mrs. Alles. But se was also be hailed! Gemer Braniski wrote on July 8, 2005: "I just read the arguments by Alles in Theologisches. It looked quite impressive and is certainly well documented. Just be thankful for this Catholic Woman that wants to end all those ridicule apparitions of Mary in her own Church. If the Catholics are serious about their religion the walls of Lourdes and Fatima has to come down!"

Dispite this support, most delineated the arguments of Frau Alles as 'balderdash', 'bunkum' and 'haver'.

The obduracy of Mrs. Alles, refusing to accept the recognition by the Church and her refusal that the Church has the right to annul previous estimations, was doomed as 'not in accordance with the facts and the history of the Church.

'Even if it might take some centuries, as was the case with Galileo'.

Let there be no doubt about the Vatican, as Mrs. Alles tries to indoctrinate in her piece. The bishop of Amsterdam extensively discussed the case of recognition during a private meeting with Cardinal Ratzinger, posterior pope Benedict XVI.

So, 'All arguments against the apparitions of the Holy Virgin in Amsterdam are merely poppycock!'

But failing in Holland and Germany didn't stop the dubious Vaak Foundation. One of the members, Nico Alles, was employed before as a banker on the Philippines.

The trick was simple: he asked his Philippine friends to send letters to their local bishop to ask about what was the meaning of the clause "that once was Mary" in the Amsterdam Blessing?

As the president of the Philippines was a great devouty to the Lady of all Peoples, this was more a political act as it had anything to do with the devotion.

Certain Bishops of the Philippines were too happy to rumble about the devotion,

Or as Biro Battere wrote on December 25, 2008: "After the church recognized the Amsterdam apparitions of the Holy Virgin, a pressure group in the Philippines misused Amsterdam for political goals. To damage president Gloria Macapagal-Arroyo, who believes her election was wrought by the Dutch apparition. A huge image of Our Lady of Amsterdam flanked her at the inauguration. So her opponents organized problems with the Prayer of Amsterdam, and more specific about how to interpret the words 'that once was Mary' in it."

The bishops of the Philippines had no idea and transferred the question to the Catholic Bishop's Conference of the Philippines (CBCP), who send the question to Rome.

It was well planned. The Head of the Congregation was just elected pope.

THE AMSTERDAM LADY IN ROME

Archbishop Angelo Amato was as secretary in charge when the letter of the bishops in the Philippines arrived.

His boss was now pope. Angelo was waiting the usual promotions made when a new pope was invested on Peters Chair. Still it was guessing who would become the new Head of the Doctrine of the Faith. But certain he was now in charge.

Amando spoke out in public against marriages between persons of the same sex and defended with fire Opus Dei when this organization was attacked in the Da Vinci Code. Said that "if such lies and errors had been directed at the Koran or the Holocaust they would have justly provoked a world uprising".

Although his former boss Benedict XVI had made no objections when Bishop Punt came to the Vatican to discuss. the official recognition of the

Amsterdam Apparitions, now Amato has taken issue with the phrase, "who once was Mary". That was news! As that clause was granted its first 'Imprimatur' already over sixty years ago.

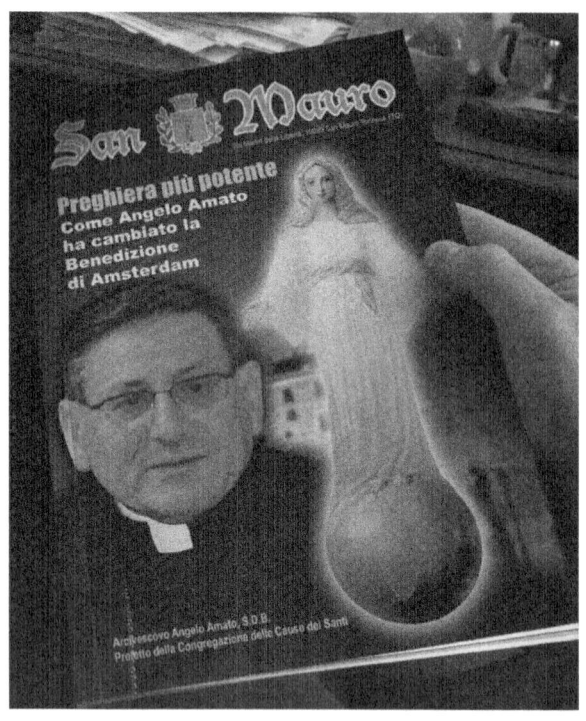

Coverstar Angelo Amato S.D.B.

Ida in 1996: "Yes, that *once was Mary*. I did not understand what it meant when Our Lady said the prayer to me. And when she came to *May the Lady of all peoples, who once was Mary* I thought: what are you saying? I called loudly: *But you are always*

Mary? But she just smiled and continued. Later she said the blessing again.

But Bishop Huibers told me that *once was Mary* was attacked, and asked me if I was sure that the Lady had said so. I answered: I also felt that it was crazy, monsignor, because I immediately reacted with: *What? But you have always been Mary?*

But this is what she had said. It was immediately written down after I repeated the Lady aloud.

I told a Marian theologian about, and he responded not to worry, as that sentence is solid as a rock. I asked how? He said: *Mary once was an ordinary girl, which lived in Jerusalem. And then she received the message that she would become pregnant of Jesus.*

But it is attacked. Until now. People come to me and ask about that *once was Mary*. And every time I have to explain it. It is like our Queen Beatrix which was first a princess before she became a queen. But for me too was it a strange sense."

Ida herself found the words strange, and the first local Church authorities to whom she had to go to obtain approval of the prayer initially gave permission only with the words "who once was Mary" omitted. This led Our Lady to insist on March 28 and July 2, 1951 and again on February 17 and April 6, 1952, that permission should be given for the publication of the prayer in its entirety. This was finally conceded and on October 5, 1952, Our

Lady told the visionary, Ida Peerdeman, to tell the Bishop that she was satisfied.

On July 2, 1951 (then observed as the Feast of the Visitation), Our Lady herself explained:

The words "who once was Mary" mean: many people have known Mary just as Mary. Now, however, in this new era which is beginning I want to be the Lady of all Peoples. Everybody will understand this.

The expression does not infer that the Lady of all Peoples is not still the historical Mary, nor does it eliminate the legitimate use of invoking the Mother of Jesus as "Mary," as in the case of the praying of the Rosary. The name of Mary is repeatedly used for Our Lady in the messages themselves (cf. October 5, 1952; December 8, 1952; May 10, 1953 messages, etc.). But it does give proper dignity and honor to Our Lady's unique human cooperation with the Redeemer and to the salvific roles granted her by God (cf. Lumen Gentium, 57-62).

As an example to illustrate the meaning of "The Lady of all Peoples, who once was Mary" we can use the case of the present pope. We could appropriately say, "Pope Benedict XVI who once was Joseph Ratzinger." The sentence identifies both the original historical identity of Benedict XVI as Joseph Ratzinger, and at the same time refers to the higher honor and dignity due to him in light of his eventual papal office and title as Vicar of Christ on earth. So too, the expression, "The Lady of all Peoples, who once was Mary" identifies the original historical identity of Mary of Nazareth, but also honors the new office and title of the "Lady of all Peoples", which is granted to her by the Divine Redeemer at Calvary.

Thus the general meaning of the expression, "The Lady of all Peoples, who once was Mary" is: The woman who first was known as Mary (and still is), is now to be universally recognized and venerated as the Lady of all Peoples.

Unfortunately Bishop Amato appeared not to understand this when he wrote to the Philippine Cardinal:

"With regard to the devotion known as 'Lady of All Nations' and the Marian apparitions experienced by the late visionary Ida Peerdeman, I wish to advise Your Excellency that although the said apparitions have received approval from His Excellency the Most Rev. Joseph Maria Punt, Bishop of Haarlem (Holland), in his Communications of 31 May 2002, the Congregation for the Doctrine of the Faith has expressed concern regarding one particular aspect of that devotion whereby official prayers invoke the Blessed Virgin as Lady of All Nations 'who was once Mary.'

Note that Amato here acts as 'the Congregation'. Strange that the Congregation seems to be unaware that this strange clause was granted its first 'Imprimatur' for over sixty years. And that since that time over seventy Bishops and Cardinals endorsed this Amsterdam Blessing.

However, even Ida once said the Amsterdam Blessing without the words. That was during the 53rd Apparition of May 31, 1957:

My spiritual director had told me that I wasn't allowed to go to St. Thomas Church that morning, nor to adoration in the evening. In addition, I was not allowed to call him that day. So I went to Holy Mass at Peace Church. All of sudden, just before Holy Communion, I clearly heard the voice of the Lady saying,

"Today do what I tell you."

I was startled by that and said inwardly, "But I promised to obey Fr. Frehe." Yet I added humbly, "But Lord, Your will be done."

That day Ida had to go somewhere by train. But the Lady commanded her to go back.

Ida: "Before I knew it, I was out of the train and standing on the platform… All of a sudden the Lady's voice resounded very loudly over the platform: "Three o'clock at the chapel!"

Ida went to St. Thomas Church that afternoon:

"At first I didn't dare go in, but suddenly it was as if someone were pushing me, as if some kind of wind or force were carrying me into the church… I suddenly saw the light appear... When I entered the chapel, I saw the Lady slowly emerging from the light. She said to me: Pray the prayer.

Then she herself began to pray the prayer, very softly and devoutly, praying it together with me. At the end, however, I heard her say 'your Advocate' instead of 'our Advocate'. At this she moved her head forward and looked at me very intently. This confused me, such that I seemed to have skipped the words ,who once was Mary', and repeated her words, 'your Advocate'."

The Mariologist that are specialized in the case of the Amsterdam Apparitions differ in how they should interpret this in the light of subsequent Amato interference in this sentence.

In Italy they think that it was what Our Lady in Amsterdam said about celibacy during the last public apparition, is talking about the Amato-prohibition.

The Lady of all Peoples said on that occasion:

"I shall come back in private for the Church and for priests, at the time which the Lord shall determine. Say that celibacy is endangered from within. But in spite of everything, the Holy Father shall uphold it."

When Ida shook her head and said that she didn't dare say this, the Lady said somewhat angrily:

"I order you to say this!"

Angelo Amato, as Secretary of the Vatican's Congregation told the members of the Catholic Bishop's Conference of the Philippines that he does not permit any Catholic community of Christ's Faithful to pray to the Mother of God under the title of 'Lady of All Nations' with the added expression 'who was once Mary'.

This was communicated to the Bishops of the Philippines, to the religious community, 'Family of

Mary,' as well as to the Bishop of Haarlem-Amsterdam, Mgr. Punt.

Angelo Amato clearly did not realize the impact of his decision. This prayer was printed over 100 million times in more than 80 languages. It was in books, beaten in copper and lapidaried in Marmora and stone. Would Catholics obey his order and block out the words 'who once was Mary' on Amsterdam Lady-monuments in Brazil, Surinam, Congo, Philippines, Indonesia, India or the Netherlands?

When the Amato-order reached the faithful, protest were launched in Italy, the Netherlands, Brazil and in Port-au-Price, Haiti.

In Brazil, Porção (Pernambuco), where the Amsterdam Blessing is engraved on a monument on top of the 4,000 ft. Mount Dunga, the reaction of Manolito Pólo was: *If Amato thinks he can change this prayer, well, let him come and I show him the way up to the monument.*

The Dutch website RK NetNieuws (Roman Catholic NetNews) questioned the sanity of Amato. The Archbishop hates Amsterdam, it was suggested, because Amato associates this city with abortion and euthanasia.

Above an image of the Amsterdam Madonna on a wall in Port-au-Price, Haiti was written. Au diable la brousse AA (To hell with scrub like AA).

In San Mauro near Turin in the north of Italy, all 1000 copies of a magazine with Angelo Amato on the cover were burned by fanatic 'defenders of the honor of Our Lady'.

A magazine with Amato on the cover was burned.

The order of Secretary Amato was not well received, that much was clear.

Mgr. Jos Punt, bishop of the Dutch diocese Haarlem-Amsterdam, issued a directive in compliance with the Amato request.

In the press release:

"The concern of the Congregation is part of a long tradition. Initially the first local Bishop, Monsignor J. Huibers, who dealt with this devotion sixty years ago, struggled with this clause.

At first he considered the removal of the clause, but upon later reflection, he accepted it and granted permission for the 'Imprimatur'.

Up to this day, the prayer has as well received the Imprimatur of approximately seventy Bishops and Cardinals worldwide.

This indicates that they saw no contradiction with any teaching of the Church.

In 1996, the Prefect of the Congregation permitted the public release of the devotion.

In 2002, the local Bishop recognized in its essence the authenticity of the apparitions.

Naturally, the Bishop contacted the Congregation and expressed his opinion on this matter. In the meantime, he has asked the authorities of the devotion to respect the pastoral concern of the Congregation by leaving out or praying silently the clause during public prayer until further notice.

The Bishop realizes "that for many people this may cause a tension between conviction and obedience," says the press release, "but he refers to the example offered by the visionary herself. Once she experienced a similar type of dilemma and then heard the following words from 'the Lady': 'obedience comes first.'

"Of course, obedience does not exclude ongoing and open dialogue on this issue", he states. Also the great and actual importance of this prayer, that asks the 'Lord Jesus Christ, Son of the Father' to send 'now' the Holy Spirit over our wounded world, completely remains."

The devotees, instead of leaving out this clause during public prayer of the Blessing of Amsterdam, now said it silently.

Amato oversees since July 2008 the approval of certified miracles in the process which leads to the canonization of saints. As per tradition, Amato is expected to be created Cardinal-Deacon around 2010.

The Angel in Japan

It was father Gabriel Heinzelmann, one of the priests of the Amsterdam Chapel, that comforted his faithful after the letter of Amato, that the angel-apparition in Akita, Japan, when he prayed the Amsterdam Blessing, stopped at the words "that once was Mary".

Akita in Japan and Amsterdam have a mystic bound! Because the apparition of Our Lady of Akita of Sister Agnes Katsuko Sasagawa was the same Lady all the way as the Lady of all Peoples that had appeared in Amsterdam to Ida Peerdeman!

The 1973 messages of the Lady of all Peoples in Akita, were approved at the Congregation for the Doctrine of the Faith in 1988 by Cardinal Joseph

Ratzinger (later Pope Benedict XVI). Sister Agnes had been totally deaf before 1973, and remained deaf until 1982, when she was cured during Sunday Mass as Our Lady had foretold in her messages.

Marian apparitions are sometimes reported along with weeping statues of the Virgin Mary. However, to date only one single example of a combined weeping statue and apparition has been approved by the Vatican and the rest have been dismissed as hoaxes. Like in 1995, after the owner of a Madonna statue that appeared to weep blood in the town of Civitavecchia in Italy refused to take a DNA test. And in 2008 church custodian Vincenzo Di Costanzo went on trial in northern Italy for faking blood on a statue of the Virgin Mary when his own DNA was matched to the blood.

암스테르담 (모든 민족들의 어머니)

발현 장소 암스테르담 (네덜란드)
발현 날짜 1945년 3월 25일 ~ 1959년 5월 31일 (15년간)
발현 목격자 이다 페르데만 (40세)
기적. 치유 1959년 5월 31일에 일련의 여러 발현들이 장엄한 환시로 끝나는데 여기서 성모님은 천상 영광 중에 나타나시고 하얀 불의 성체로부터 온갖 광채와 장엄함 안에서 주님의 형상이 나타났다. 이때부터 발현 목격자는 미사 중에 많은 체험과 환시를 보게 되었으며 이 체험들은 "성체적 체험"이라고 불린다. 이것은 1980년까지 계속되었다.
발현지 특성 새로운 상본과 기도문 주심.
상본은 그려졌고 상본과 기도문은 교회 당국에 의해 인준되었으며 기도문은 전 세계에 50개 이상의 국어로 번역되고 수 천 만장의 카드가 여러 나라로 전파
조사 과정 암스테르담 하아를렘의 주교 보메스 몬시뇰은 하느님의 어머니를 '모든 민족들의 어머니'라는 호칭으로 공경함, 공적 봉헌 인가 성명 발표.
공동구속자, 중개자 및 변호자라는 마리아의 역할을 규정하는 새롭고 최종적인 교의를 선포해달라고 교황 성하께 요청하는 거대한 국제 운동이 교회 내에서 일어났었다.
공인 날짜 2002년 3월 31일 (57년 후)

THE AMSTERDAM APPARITIONS

Anyway, to date the only one single combined weeping statue and apparition that has been approved by the Vatican is Our Lady of Akita, and the

Amsterdam Blessing is the one and only prayer in the Holy Roman Catholic Church with one clause to be prayed in silence after secretary Angelo Amato's intervention. It gave quite a confusion.

The burning of a magazine with the effigy of Amato in Italy attracted the attention of His Holiness, pope Benedict, who wondered what was going on.

The pope himself was certain involved in the case as it was the last official approval of Marian Apparitions by the Roman Catholic Church.

To some, like the Dutch author Robert Lemm, it is most likely that the Apparitions of Amsterdam will be the very last approved in the history the Roman Catholic Church.

Not Amato but William Joseph Levada from Long Beach, California, was appointed on May 13, 2005 successor of Cardinal Ratzinger. The new Head of the Congregation for the Doctrine of the Faith resigned as Archbishop of San Francisco effective August 17, 2005. He was elevated to the cardinalate in 2006. As a result of his elevation, Cardinal Levada is now eligible to participate in any future papal conclaves that begin before his 80th birthday on June 15, 2016.

As the most influential position in the government of the Church apart from the Holy Father himself, Levada is considered the highest ranking American in the institution and considered a possible successor to Pope Benedict XVI, as he is in the same position as Cardinal Joseph Ratzinger.

Bill Levada was not unknown to the Roman Curia nor the case of the Lady of all Peoples, as he was an official of the Congregation for the Doctrine of the Faith from 1976 to 1982. Where he served under Paul VI, John Paul I, and John Paul II and under Franjo Seper and Joseph Ratzinger as prefects of the CDF. In November 2000, Levada was appointed one of the members of the CDF, where he again served under Ratzinger.

In addition to his position as Prefect of the CDF, Cardinal Levada is the president of the Pontifical Biblical Commission and the International Theological Commission and member in the Congregation for Bishops, the Congregation for the Causes of Saints, the Congregation for the Evangelization of Peoples, the Pontifical Council for

Promoting Christian Unity and the Pontifical Commission Ecclesia Dei.

The Vatican's Congregation for the Doctrine of the Faith issued and published on May 29, 2008, in the Vatican newspaper L'Osservatore Romano, a decree signed by Cardinal Levada, as Prefect of the Congregation, on the existing ban on women priests by asserting that women priests and the bishops who ordain them would be excommunicated "latae sententiae".

As Prefect of the Congregation for the Doctrine of the Faith, Levada is the principal defender of all the moral and theological doctrines of the Roman Catholic Church, sometimes acting as chief prosecutor against members of the Church who have strayed from those values. Cardinal Levada's views mostly reflect the official teachings of the Roman Catholic Church.

In January 2009 Pope Benedict XVI issued new guidelines on distinguishing between real or 'demonic' visions of Mary.

You don't have to be a clairvoyance to see that the new procedure is a copycat of the procedure that was followed in the case of Ida Peerdeman and the Amsterdam Apparitions. And that Ida would pass this new examination with flying colors.

According the new guidelines the local bishop will need to set up a commission of psychiatrists, psychologists, theologians and priests when a claim of heavenly apparitions occurs. Those claims will be investigated systematically.

The first step will be to impose silence on the alleged visionaries and if they refuse to obey then this will be taken as a sign that their claims are false.

The visionaries will next be visited by psychiatrists, either atheists or Catholics, to certify their mental health and to verify whether they are suffering from conditions of a hysterical or hallucinatory character or from delusions of leadership.

The third step will be to investigate the person's level of education and to determine if they have had access to material that could be used to falsely support their claims.

If the visionary is considered credible they will ultimately be questioned by one or more demonologists and exorcists to exclude the possibility that Satan is hiding behind the apparitions in order to deceive the faithful.

The handbook comes six years after the Pope - when he was Cardinal Joseph Ratzinger –said that such phenomena posed a risk to the unity of the Church. It will be published by the Congregation for the Doctrine of the Faith.

May 31, 2008

A major Marian conference on approved Marian Apparitions was held at the historic Victoria Hotel in Park Plaza in Amsterdam on the anniversary of the last apparition of Our Lady of all Peoples on May 31, 1959 in the presence of 100 selected guests.

Our Lady of Amsterdam with Joachim Cardinal Meisner on the stage where stars like Michael Jackson, U2 or Bob Dylan used to perform.

This day was a landmark to all confused by the campaign against the Amsterdam Apparitions. No doubt about the position of The Lady of all Peoples inside the Roman Catholic Church, as her effigy was extensively incensed by Joachim Cardinal

Meisner. Archbishop of Worlds richest diocese and a very close friend of Pope Benedict XVI.

You think Cardinal Meisner would come when there was something 'fishy' with the Amsterdam Apparitions, as suggested by the very few, but very loud present opponents. It was the largest gathering of Catholics in Germany since the visit of the Pope himself.

The Mother of all Nations was venerated as a Superstar in Germany's largest indoor-complex, the Arena of Cologne. In the spotlight on the same stage where stars like Michael Jackson, U2 or Bob Dylan used to perform. On this day just the image of the Amsterdam Apparition was enough.

Dear reader,

We tried to do our best, but if you have any comment or suggestions concerning this book or know linguistic corrections, please, let us know, so we can make this book better for the next readers.

Mail to:

mokumtv@gmail.com
at the attention of TeleBooks.

From the press:
Silenced prayers in the Diocese of Fresno

FRESNO CITY - (RC NetNews) Jose Dominguez, chairman of the Knights of the Lady of all People of Clovis (Fresno City, California) announced that the Knights will pray the Silenced Version of the miraculous Amsterdam Blessing 4 times in 2009.

The "Right to remain silence in prayer" is an initiative of a group from the Cathedral of St. Vibiana in Los Angeles, to comfort those that will say The Amsterdam Blessing as Our Lady herself has told, but also will show obedience to William Joseph Cardinal Levada. This head of Congregation for the Doctrine of the Faith in the Roman Curia changed some words in the Amsterdam formula, after these caused uproar in the Philippines.

Jose Dominguez: "*You can't change words in a supernatural Prayer. If you do so, it doesn't work any longer.*"

The first Silenced Amsterdam Blessing will be said at Our Lady of Perpetual Help on Sunday, January 4 2009, after the service of 8:00 a.m.

The prayer will also be said on Sunday, May 11, Friday, August 15 and on Monday, December 8 after the Misa en Español at 8:00 a.m. We are planning to invite Fr. Salvador Gonzalez, Jr. , Director of Vocations for the diocese, to assists in the Amsterdam vocation of Monday, December 8. The Church of Our Lady is located at 9th and Dewitt Streets in Downtown Clovis - 3 blocks south of Bullard and 3 blocks east of Clovis Avenue.

(RC NetNews, December 2008).

THE MOTHER OF ALL NATIONS

The Apparitions Of Our Lady in Amsterdam

Who is Who

Amato, Angelo S.D.B. Archbishop (8-6-1938) Prefect of the Congregation for the Causes of Saints since 9 July 2008. On 19 December 2002 appointed as Secretary of the Congregation for the Doctrine of the Faith and served under Cardinals Joseph Ratzinger (Benedict XVI in 2005) and William Levada between 2005 and 2008. In the lull between Ratzinger and Levada he prohibited the Philippine Bishops to pray to the 'Lady of All Nations' with the added expression 'who was once Mary', although Cardinal Ratzinger agreed in 1996 with Mgr. Bomers, Bishop of Haarlem, that there was no objection against this Blessing of Amsterdam, that since 1951 enjoyed Church approval.

Auclair, Raoul (Ambrault, France 4-3-1906 - Quebec City 8-1-1997) On February 19, 1966, Raoul gave a conference at the Théâtre du Tertre in Paris, devoted to Mary's apparitions at Amsterdam. Since 1978 joined the Army of as editor at "Les Éditions Stella". In 1982 - a new revised and enlarged edition of his *La Dame de Tous les Peuples – Ouverture à l'intelligence des messages* was published.

Benedict XVI, see Ratzinger.

Bomers, Henricus Joseph Aloysius CM (Groenlo, 19-4-1936 - Haarlem 12-9-1998). Bishop of Haarlem 1983-1998. Granted the permission for the public veneration of the Amsterdam Apparition under the title Lady of all Peoples on May 31, 1996.

Wolfgang Brenninkmeijer (1913-1977).

Brenninkmeijer, Wolfgang (Berlin 24-5-1923 – Amsterdam 10-1-1977). President C&A. Together with his mother Gertrud a great benefactors of the Amsterdam Apparitions. Married to May Pessers. No children.

Brouwer, Herman A.A. (Eindhoven 26-9-1924 - Zeist 27-10-2008). Chairman of the Lady of all Peoples Foundation.

Callandhout, Rien van. Pastor Thomaschurch Amsterdam at the time of the Apparitions.

Colin, Michel (1905-1974). Tried to kidnap the Amsterdam Apparitions after he visited Ida Peerdeman. Ordained a priest in 1935, but reduced to the lay state in 1951. Claimed to be crowned Pope Clement XV by the Archangels on October 7, 1950 in the French village of Clémery. Pope Pius XII declared him a *vitandus* (one who should be avoided).

Deursen, H.J. Rector Grootseminarie Warmond. Member of the Commission 1955, the first to investigate the Amsterdam Apparitions.

Dodewaard, Joannes Antonius Eduardus van (1960-1966) From 1960-66 Bishop of Haarlem.

Franken, Rudo (Eindhoven). Chaplain in Echt 1985, Heythuysen 1987, Pastor in Weert-Groenewoud 1989, Roggel 1998, later transferred to Mook. Clarinet player and author of two books on Hernia and Medjugorje. Founder/Chairman of the Vaak Foundation against the Amsterdam Apparitions.

Frehe, Mathias (Thijs) Josephus Jacobus Paulus (Nijmegen 10-1-1890 – Alkmaar 12-2-1967). Spiritual director of Ida Peerdeman.

Thijs Frehe, first Spiritual director of Ida Peerdeman.

Gaag, J. van der, Deacon of Amsterdam. Member of the Commission 1955, the first to investigate the Amsterdam Apparitions.

Geukers, Mgr. G.P.M. Vicaris-general Haarlem. Member of the Commission 1955, the first to investigate the Amsterdam Apparitions.

Giguère, Marie-Paule. (Sainte-Germaine-du-Lac-Etchemin 14-9-1921). Kidnapped the Lady of all Peoples. Founded in 1971 The Community of the Lady of All Nations in Quebec Canada. Constituted in 1975 as a Pious Association by Maurice Cardinal Roy, Archbishop of Quebec and Primate of Canada. In 2007, the Congregation for the Doctrine of the Faith excommunicated the group for heretical teachings and beliefs. Miss Giguère married in 1944 and had five children: André (1945), Louise (1947), Michèle (1948) Pierre (1950) and Danielle (1952).

Hnilica, Pavol (30-3-1921 - 8-10- 2006) was a Slovak Roman-Catholic bishop, Jesuit and old friend of Pope John Paul II. He was a clandestine priest and bishop. In 1952 he fled from Slovakia and studied and worked mainly in Rome and Fatima. Organizer of National Prayerdays to the Amsterdam Apparitions in 2001 in Ireland, Austria, Switzerland, England, Germany, Holland and Slovakia.

Huibers, Johannes Petrus - Bishop (Amsterdam 15-11-1875 - Heemstede 20-4-1969).

Kerssemakers. Johannes (Jan) Petrus Lambertus s.s.s., (Eindhoven 2-1-1923 – Amsterdam 3-23-1981). Spiritual Director of Ida Peerdeman.

Korse, Piet (Amandus O.F.M.). (1910). Performed Last Sacrament to Ida Peerdeman.

Kuipers, Dr. Harry. Vicar-General of the Bishop of Haarlem till 1985, later Broadcast pastor in Amersfoort. Chairman of a commission of nine members that started a third investigation in 1972. The findings were presented to the Holy Office.

Leechburch Auwers, J.A.A. (Jan). (1923) Director of a publishing house and parliamentary employee of a small Roman Catholic party in the Netherlands. At his 81st year headed the election list for European Parliament.

Leeman, Arnold (Nol), Chairman Lady of all Nation Foundation Amsterdam since 1996.

Lemm, Robert C.J. (Rotterdam 7-5-1945). Author several influential books about the Lady of all Peoples; translator laureate Martinus-Nijhoff-Prize.

Levada, William Joseph (Long Beach, California 15-6-1936) Appointed successor of Ratzinger May 13, 2005 as Head of the Congregation for the Doctrine of the Faith. In 2006 Bill Levada suggested Bishop Punt that if people don't understand the clause 'that once was Mary' should pray 'the Holy Virgin Mary'.

Lierde, Mgr Dr Petrus (Piet) Canisius J. van (1907-Roeselaere 13-3-1995). Augustine, Sacrista and Vicario Generale di Sua Santita (Vicar General of His Holiness) in Rome from 1951 till 1991. The five popes he has served, he once characterized as follows: Pius XII (1958) a hard worker and strong administrator. John XXIII (1963), generous and friendly. Paul VI (1978), suffer from the office and often is coming back to earlier made decisions. John Paul I (1978) very engaging. John Paul II (1978) someone with a strong desire to eliminate the exaggerations of the Vatican.

Meeteren, Theresia van. Worked for the Lady of all Nation Foundation Amsterdam at the end of Ida's life.

Meysing, C.N., Pastor, who gave the image of the Amsterdam Apparition as painted by Heinrich Repke its first imprimatur: Wassenaar 2-6-1951 Censor a.b. dep.

Peerdeman, Isje (Ida) Johanna (Alkmaar 13-8-1905 – Amsterdam 17-6-1996). To her Our Lady of Amsterdam appeared between 1945 and 1959.

Peerdeman, Pieter (Piet) Jacobus (Alkmaar - 2-2-1964). Brother of Ida, married to Afra Bos. Son:

Jan Peerdeman, daughter Helena van der Heijden-Peerdemans.

Peerdeman, Gesina (Ge) J. (Alkmaar 13-8-1897 – Amsterdam 1-9-1980). Sister of Ida.

Peerdeman, Johanna (Jo) M. (Alkmaar 6-6-1899 – Amsterdam 1-9-1990), Sister of Ida. Married to Groothues Heidkamp.

Peerdeman, Geertruida (Truus) E. (Alkmaar 5-10-1900 – Amsterdam 19-3-1994). Sister of Ida.

Peerdeman, Helena (Leentje) (1879 - Amsterdam 18-7-1914). Mother of Ida.

Peerdeman, Rembert (- Amsterdam 17-6-1934). Father of Ida, textile merchant.

Perquin-Gerris, dra. Jeanne Marie ('s-Hertogenbosch 9-3-1919). Added to the Commission 1955 to investigate the Amsterdam Apparitions.

Peeters, Wim. Pressman Bishop Punt of Haarlem-Amsterdam.

Punt, Joseph (Jos) Marianus. (Alkmaar 10-1-1946). Punt became a priest on June 9, 1979 and auxiliary bishop of Diocese of Haarlem in 1995. On July 21, 2001 he was appointed bishop of Haarlem and concluded a period of half a century of investigation, and declared the Amsterdam apparitions to be of a supernatural origin.

Ratzinger, Joseph Alois (16-4-1927) Succeeded Pope John Paul II on 19 April 2005 as Benedict XVI. After a long career as an internationally noted academic, serving as a professor at various German universities, he was appointed Archbishop of Munich and Freising and cardinal in 1977. In 1981, he settled in Rome when he became Prefect of the Congregation for the Doctrine of the Faith. Agreed 1996 with Mgr. Bomers, Bishop of Haarlem, that there is no objection against the public veneration of the Blessed Virgin under this title Lady of all Peoples nor the Blessing of Amsterdam, that since 1951 enjoyed Church approval by Mgr. Huibers. This was overruled by Archbishop Angelo Amato in 2005 and repaired by Cardinal William Levada in 2006.

Repke, Heinrich (Werne 31-3-1877 – Rheda-Wiedenbrück 25-12-1962). German painter that painted in 1951 the first known image of the Lady of all Peoples in his atelier in Wiedenbrück in North Rhineland-Westphalia. With over 100 million copies printed in 2009 by far the best distributed painter of our age.

Šeper, Franjo. (Osijek 2-10-1905 – Rome 30-12-1981). Croatian Cardinal and Prefect of the Congregation for the Doctrine of the Faith from 1968 to 1981. He had advocated religious liberty and the introduction of the vernacular into the liturgy during the Second Vatican Council. Šeper was the author of the document Mysterium Ecclesiae. Cardinal Šeper retired as Prefect on 25 November 1981 and died a month later from a heart attack. He is buried in Zagreb beside the tomb of Cardinal Stepinac.

Sigl, Paul Maria (Natters, Austria 22-10-1949). Spiritual Director of the Familia of Mary and assistant of the late Slovak Bishop Pavel Hnilica.

Smet, J. de. Psychiatrist and director Sint Willibrordusstichting Heiloo. Head of commission 1955, the first to investigate the Apparitions of Amsterdam, as reported 7-4-1956, with an advisory addition by Dr. Perquin.

Soffner, Raphaël. (Hollandia, Irian Jaya 4-8-1962) Head of the Commission that cleared the way for the official recognition of the Amsterdam Apparitions in 2002.

Steur, Dr. Klaas. (Volendam 23-6-1905 - Volendam 28-7-1985) Professor of Theology in Warmond, author of 31 books. Was consulted about the theological substance of the Amsterdam Blessing in 1955 by the bishop of Haarlem. In December 1954 was forced to leave the seminar where he was teaching. In 1964 he became Pastor in De Zilk.

Schweigman O.P., Dr. F.A. Dominican Provincial who gave the Amsterdam Blessing its first approval: imprimatur Neomagi 1-5-1951 Libr. Censor.

Willebrands, dr. Johannes Gerardus Maria (Bovenkarspel, 4-9-1909 - Denekamp, 2-8-2006), member of the Commission 1955, the first to investigate the Amsterdam Apparitions. Willebrands served as President of the Pontifical Council for Promoting Christian Unity from 1969 to 1989, was Archbishop of Utrecht from 1975 to 1983. Elevated to the cardinalate in 1969, Willebrands was considered papabile at the two conclaves held in 1978. Moved to a Franciscan convent in 1997, where he died age 96 as oldest living member of the College of Cardinals.

Zaal, Jannie. Aid to Ida Peerdeman at the end of her life.

Zwartkruis, Theodorus Henricus Johannes (1966-1983). Bishop of Haarlem 1966-1983.

Some of the places where the Amsterdam Apparition is venerated

Austria, Kolsass

Aktionszentrum Frau aller Völker Österreich
Peter Jaist Weg
A-6114 Kolsass

Argentina, Lujan

There is an image of the Lady of all Peoples in the crypt of the National Basilica in Lujan

Belgium, Tienen

Michel Vanwinckel has experienced a great deal of support and help from the Lady of all Peoples. For this reason, he has erected a little chapel in his garden to honor Her.

This chapel at the Werkmanssteeg 21 was consecrated on September 8, 2004 is open to everyone, at all times.

Birma (Myanmar), Nyaunglebin

Chapel for the Amsterdam Lady of all Peoples in Nyaunglebin about 95 miles from Yangon in Myanmar.

Brasil, Poção (Vale do Ipojuca) Pernambuco

In Poção (Vale do Ipojuca) in the Brasilian state of Pernambuco on the top of the chapada Monte Dunga is the monument *De la Señora de todos los Pueblos y del Espíritu Santo*.

With a huge portrait of the Amsterdam Apparition.

Brazil, Atibaia

In the church of the Lady of all Peoples in Atibaia images of Our Lady are venerated, originating from six different places where Mary appeared, including the image of the Lady of all Peoples.

Central African Republic, Penge

Chapel of the Lady of all Peoples in Penge

Congo, Bonkozi

A little Church with the Image of Amsterdam was consecrated in 1993 in Bokonzi in the diocese of Budjala.

France, Ville d'Avray

A very important spot in the cult around the Mother of all Peoples is Ville d'Avray near Paris. In 1966, the miraculous painting of the Amsterdam Madonna was transferred from the cellar of the Amsterdam Thomaschurch at the request of a Dutch pastor, to the church of Ville d'Avray, département

Hauts-de-Seine near Paris for a year. Here the image was visited by violin master Yehudi Menuhin.

Germany, Schopfheim

Aktionszentrum Frau aller Völker
Deutschland und Schweiz
Kapellenstrasse 1-a
D-79650 Schopfheim

Germany, Mettingen

In Mettingen (Germany) the Amsterdam visionary Ida Peerdeman had some of the most spectacular visions of the Holy Virgin Mary.

It was the mother of the late C&A president Wolfgang Brenninkmeijer who had the now worldwide famous painting of the apparition painted!

Before it came to Amsterdam it was venerated in the private chapel of the Brenninkmeyer-family.

Mettingen, Haus Langebruck, the historic headquarter of the Brenninkmeijer family.

India, Trivandrum

Action Committee of the Lady of All Nations
16/181 Easwaravilasom Road
Trivandrum - 695 014
Kerala India

India, Trivandrum

Lady of All Nations Pilgrimage Centre
Lokmatha
Vimalapuram Thachottukavu
Peyad P.O.
Trivandrum - 695 573
Kerala India

Indonesia, Bogor

Church in honor of the Lady of all Peoples in his
diocese, Bogor, has been finished in 2007.

Indonesia, Nusa Dua, Bali

Church of The Lady of all Peoples, Jl. Bukit Kampial, Komplek Puja Mandala in the district of Nusa
Dua forms part of a complex of 4 other places of
worship of differing faiths (Muslim, Buddhist,
Hindu and Protestant). The Lady of all Peoples is a
sub parish church of the Saint Francis Xavier
Church located in Kuta. As it is located within the
tourist district the church attracts not only the residents of the area but also visitors to Bali.

Italy, Bologna

The Lady of all Peoples is solemnly exposed every day from 7:30 a.m. to 6 p.m. in the Chapel of the Blessed Sacrament.

This Chapel is maintained by the order Ancelle del S.Cuore di Gesù, via S.Stefano 63 Bologna.

Italy, Scanello

On May 31, 2008 don Massimo Pelliconi enthroned a statue of the Lady of all Peoples in the parish church of Scanello, near Loiano (diocese of Bologna).

Italy, Cecchina di Ariccia

Casa 'Signora di tutti i Popoli'
Via Nettunense, 31 A
I 00040 Cecchina di Ariccia

Italy, Florence

Stainglass window in the Lady of all Peoples chapel in Pieve di Sant Ilario in Montereggi (Fiesole).

Italy, Rieti

In November 1999 an image of the Lady of all Peoples was placed in the 13th century 'Hermitage of the Most Holy Cross' deep in the forest on the Colli di Amatrice. To visit the inside of the hermitage you have to contact the pastor of Scai, as it is rarely open.

Italy, Turin

Colle della Maddalena
Tifosi di Signora di tutti i Popoli
Montly Amsterdam Blessing between Faro della
Vittoria and Castelgomberto on the Colle della
Maddalena.

Italy, San Mauro Torinese

Via Giacomo Matteotti, San Mauro Torinese.

Italy, Capri

An image of the Lady of all Peoples is enthroned in
the Hermitage of Santa Maria a Cetrella.

Thousands of people took to the streets of Limerick in a mass demonstration against gangland violence in the city after the death of Roy Collins. Photograph: Paul Collins

The Irish Times 14-7-2009

Ireland, Limerick

Lady of All Nations Action Centre
Old Pallas House
Old Pallas
Co. Limerick

Japan, Tokyo

Subete No Tami
No Onhaha Fukuyu No Kai
MBE-254, 3-28, Kioicho,
Chiyoda-ku, Tokyo,
102-8557, Japan

Japan, Akita

Here is the 1963 famous statue of the Lady of all Peoples that had shed tears.

奇跡

アムステルダムからの元の水

Amsterdam Water.

Netherlands, Amsterdam

Chapel of the Lady of All Nations
The Brenninkmeijer Villa
Diepenbrockstraat 3
1077 VX Amsterdam

In the 1970s, the Foundation of the Lady of All Peoples took over the C&A Brenninkmeijer possession at Diepenbrockstreet for a symbolic price. A chapel, barely visible, was established there. Left of the altar, the painting of the Lady of All Peoples.

There was also a secretariat, where Ida Peerdeman spent the last years of her life Neighbor was the first president of the European Bank, Willem Duisenberg.

Netherlands, Velsen-Noord

In the Saint Joseph Church in Velsen-Noord.

Netherlands, Ameland

On marketdays in Nes an image of the Lady of all Peoples is placed in the Heilige Hoek (Holy Corner) next to the portal of the Reformed Church at Kerksplein.

Netherlands, Zwarte Haan

Amsterdam Blessing Prayergroup-walk 1st Fridays starts in St. Annaparochie, through Nij Altoenae.

Nigeria, Otukpo

In the diocese Otukpo.

Philippines, Cebu

Chapel for the Amsterdam Lady of all Peoples with a Waterwell is build by the local Confraternity of the Lady of all Peoples.

Philippines, Bohol

Shrine of the Lady of all Peoples.

Philippines, Makati City

The Lady of all Peoples
P.O.Box (8) 814
Dasmarinas Village
1222 Makati City,
Philippines

Philippines, Dagumbaan

Shrine of the Lady of all Peoples.

Philippines, Bibincahan

Chapel in honor of the Lady of all Peoples built by Mrs. Sally Lee.

Sally became Mayor of Sorsogon City with the intervention of the Amsterdam Lady of all Peoples.

Philippines, Iloilo

Shrine of the Lady of all Peoples.

Philippines, Gango

Shrine of the Lady of all Peoples.

Philippines, Lipa

Shrine of the Lady of all Peoples.

Philippines, Negros

Shrine of the Lady of all Peoples.

Philippines, Siquijor

Shrine of the Lady of all Peoples.

Poland, Kiczarowo

Holy Family church in Kiczarowo

Poland, Stargard Szczecinski

Chapel in the presbytery in Saint Joseph's parish in
Stargard Szczecinski

Spain, Barcelona

In the parish church Santa María de Gracia in Bar-
celona P. Jaime Dasquens Solé enthroned an image
of the Lady of all Peoples on October 12, 2005.

Surinam, Paramaribo

In Paramaribo, Surinam, the prayer of Amsterdam is beautifully depicted on the outer wall of the church of the Holy Redeemer, situated at the Schietbaanweg.

Surinam, Groningen

His Excellency, Bishop Jozef Maria Punt consecrated a Lady of all Peoples shrine in Groningen on August 23, 2008.

Switzerland, Wallis

In the chapel consecrated to St. Wendelin in Findeln, Staldenried, the Lady of all Peoples is depicted in one of the five stainglass windows

Switzerland, St. Gallen

Painting of Amsterdam Madonna by Peter Büser in the Lapidarium of the abbey of St. Gall.

Switzerland, Ticino

Small free standing memorial made of granite with the Lady of all Peoples was consecrated on September 8, 2002.

Trinidad

The Archbishop of Port of Spain His Grace Edward Gilbert consecrated on June 1, 2008, the Lady of all Peoples Church in D'Abadie Trinidad.

USA, St. Louis

Lady of all Peoples Action Center
P.O. Box 31481
St. Louis, MO 63131 USA

USA, Pembroke Pines, Florida

In the St. Edward Catholic Church in Pembroke Pines, Florida, hangs an image of the Lady of all Peoples with 63 flags.

USA, Wyandotte, Michigan

Stanislaus Kostka parish in Wyandotte, Michigan.

Amsterdam busstop, 2009.

Ida Peerdeman, 3 years old.

The young Ida Peerdeman
at the time of the demonic attacks.

Zieneres mej. Peerdeman (rechts) en 2 vriendinnen
...werktuig in hemels spel... HP 24 DEC 65

Visionary miss Peerdeman (right) and two ladyfriends
...tool in heavenly game... Haagse Post 25-12-1965.

Ida Peerdeman in 1971.

The Lady of all Nations
from the Heinrich Repke painting.

The Lady of all Nations
with a 'Yiddish' headscarf.

Sursum Corda

MMIX Edition St. Louis, MO - $ 4.50

St Maria Faustina

THE AMSTERDAM APPARITIONS
Fr. Paul Maria Sigl
makes it move!

Sursum Corda Edition 2009
The Lady with the Repke headscarf, Saint Maria-Faustina Kowalska
with an international cap and Father Sigl baldheaded.

Amsterdam Spaarndammerbuurt
The Lady with a 'Yiddish' headscarf.

Amsterdam Nieuwmarkt
The Lady with the Repke headscarf.

144

Map for pilgrims to Amsterdam
The Lady with a 'Yiddish' headscarf.

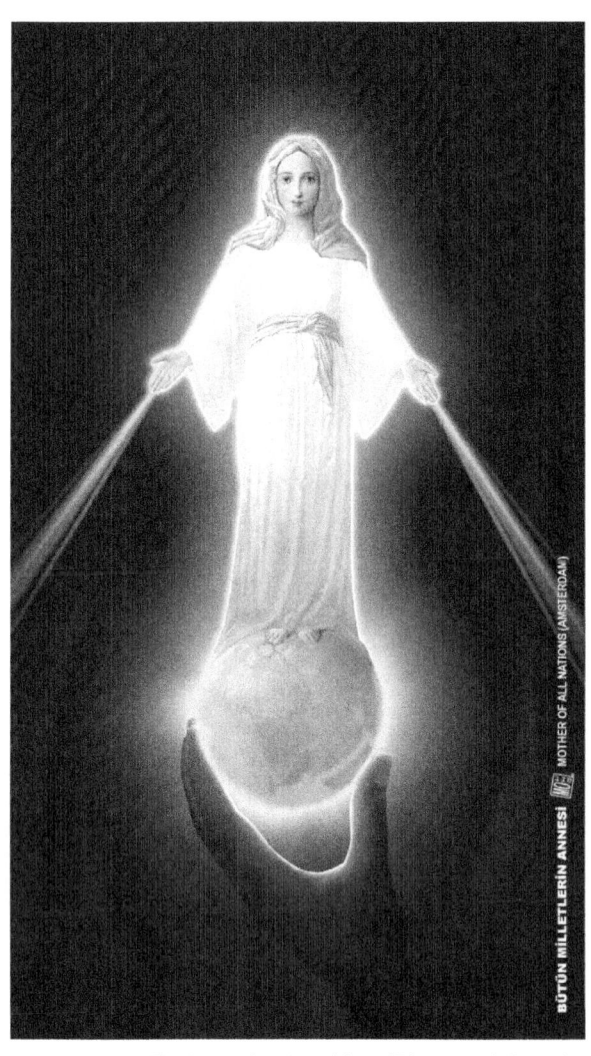

BÜTÜN MİLLETLERİN ANNESİ · MOTHER OF ALL NATIONS (AMSTERDAM)

The Amsterdam Apparition of The Lady of all Peoples
The Lady with a 'Yiddish' headscarf.

Fatima and Amsterdam, bilocate apparition of Our Lady in 1917
The Lady of Fatima with an international headscarf.

The Lady of all Peoples above an Amsterdam canal
The Lady with the Repke headscarf.

Selfadhesive of the Lady of all Peoples on a busstop in Frisia
The Lady with the Repke headscarf.

The Lady of all Peoples on a busstop in Frisia
The Lady with the Repke headscarf.

Self-adhesive of The Lady of all Peoples:
Crime stops where Mary apparite!

The Lady with the Repke headscarf.

Друзья дамы
всех
людей

Russian Friends of the Amsterdam Lady.

ANDENKENAUSGABE

MariaBode

Die Frau aller Völker

Maria in Deutschland

Die schönste Marienerscheinungen

MariaBode special German edition 2009
The Lady with the Repke headscarf.

First Apparition of **The Lady of all Nations**
13 October 1917, Langestraat, Amsterdam

Illustration from the MariaBode
The Lady with a 'Yiddish' headscarf.

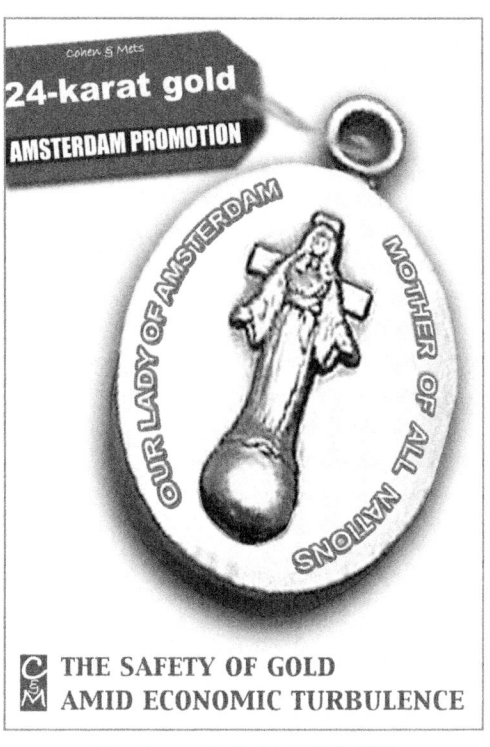

Advertisement in the MariaBode 2009
The Lady with the Repke headscarf.

L'OSSERVATORE ROMANO

GIORNALE QUOTIDIANO — POLITICO RELIGIOSO

Una saggia natura · Non praevalebunt

Ora è il tempo che il mondo sta aspettando un nuovo Lourdes?

La chiesa riconosce le apparizioni de Amsterdam

Come seguir Jesus in questo mondo

La Sua passione li ha salvati!

Nuovi Miracoli

Nostre Informazioni

Special Edition 2002
The Lady with the Repke headscarf.

Our Lady on a painting of Saenredam, a Dutch Master
The Lady with the Repke headscarf.

The Amsterdam Apparition is inspiring the greatest artists.

Postcard, Rome 2009
The Lady with the Repke headscarf.

Advertisement Royal Dutch Airlines in MariaBode 2009:
If you fly to Amsterdam, fly with KLM.

The Lady with a 'Yiddish' headscarf.

The divine Lady of all Peoples
The Lady with the Repke headscarf.

Painting 1958
The Lady with the Repke headscarf.

Say the Amsterdam Blessing – Talking keychain with all 3 versions:
The original, the Amato-silenced and the Levada/Vatican renewed
style.

The Lady with the Repke headscarf.

Solemn adoration of the Amsterdam Madonna, 2002
The Lady with the Repke headscarf.

Films with the Amsterdam Virgin

Mary in the Quran

Dutch language documentary Maria in de Koran (Mary in the Quran) has as *extra* on the DVD the MokumTV interview with Ida Peerdeman, incl. footage of Ida's funeral, Bishop Punt explaining his approval of the Amsterdam apparition to Muslims during a Ramadan-iftar and an interview with author Robert Lemm in Ephese. This film spread the knowledge about the Amsterdam apparition to an audience that quite possibly had never seen the inside of a Roman Catholic Church.

I Amsterdam en de Moeder van alle Volkeren

Massale belangstelling voor de documentaire van Mohamed el-Fers tijdens een bijeenkomst van fans van de Amsterdamse Mariaverschijningen in de Hollandhal van de Amsterdamse RAI afgelopen week.

Première: 12-9-2004 Ketelhuis Amsterdam
DVD 60:00 minutes Region free PAL
Producer: Veyis Güngör
Director: Mohamed el-Fers
Türkevi DVD 04-4 2004
Language: Dutch
Screen: 4:3
Sound: Dolby
Subtitles: none

Ave Maria

Dutch language feature documentary Ave Maria by feminist filmmaker Nouchka van Brakel (1940). traveled to Turkey, Poland, Spain and The Netherlands. With interview Bishop Punt about the Amsterdam apparition, the International Prayerday in the Amsterdam RAI and footage from the Mother Mary House in Ephese.

Première: 07-12-2006 Camera/Studio Utrecht
DVD 70:00 minutes Region 2 PAL
Producer: Eyeworks Egmond Documentary and
KRO Television the Netherlands
Director: Nouchka van Brakel
Homescreen DVD December 2006
Language: Dutch
Screen: 16:9 anamorphic
Sound: Dolby Digital 2.0
Subtitles: Dutch, English

The messages of the Lady of all People

Telefilm in Malayalam language produced in India by Messolans Films, in association with the Foundation of the Lady of all Peoples, Amsterdam. Highlighting Ida's life, her great love for God and the startling way in which Our Lady revealed the future to her with unmistakable clarity and the understanding that our God is a God of Mercy and Grace.

Première: 15-8-2009 Trivandrum, India
Telefilm 45:00 minutes
Producer: Messolans Films, in association with the

Foundation of the Lady of All Nations, Amsterdam. Language: Malayalam (upcoming 2010 English edition)
Screen: 4:3

Ida

Upcoming 2011 animated film, "Ida", produced in the Netherlands by MokumTV of Amsterdam. Portraying the supernatural and extraordinary mystical experiences in Ida's life as animated feature. Based on the voice-recordings of Ida Peerdeman of the interviews by Mohamed el-Fers.

Bibliography

Alles, Hildegard (2008). De Vrouwe van alle Volkeren. Hilversum: St.Vaak. ISBN 978-90-9023172-3

Alles, N.H. (1999). Amsterdam. Hilversum: St. Vaak

Arons, Ed (12-8-2005). Kritiek op "de Vrouwe"'. Eindhoven: Katholiek Nieuwsblad

Analecta diocese Haarlem, (1956). 1 May 1956. Hilversum: Gooi en Sticht BV

Analecta diocese Haarlem, (1973). Nr. 1-2, March 2 1973. Hilversum: Gooi en Sticht BV

Baum, Hans (1970). Die apokalyptische Frau aller Völker. Kommentare zu den Amsterdamer Erscheinungen und Prophezeiungen. Stein am Rhein

Benedict XVI see Ratzinger

Bernardo, Antonio (1988). Berndette recounts het Apparitions. Lourdes: Editions André Doucet et Fils

Blackbourn, David (1994). Marpingen: Apparitions of the Virgin Mary in Nineteenth-Century Germany. New York: Alfred A. Knopf. ISBN 0-679-41843-1

Bouflet, Joachim (2000). Faussaires de Dieu (Falsifiers of God). Paris: Edition des Presses de la Renaissance. ISBN 2-85-61669-70

Brown, Michael H. (1998). The Last Secret. Ann Arbor, Michigan: Charis. ISBN 1-57918-339-5

Brouwer, H.A. a.a. (1967). De boodschap van de Vrouwe van Alle Volkeren. Amsterdam: Comité 'Vrouwe van alle Volkeren'

Brouwer, H.A. (1995). In het licht van de Vrouwe van alle Volkeren. Zeist: Comité

Brouwer a.a., H.A. (2008). De mondiale zegetocht van de Vrouwe van Alle Volkeren. Zeist: eigen beheer

Bruggemeijer, Pater Bé (1967). In memoriam Mathias J. Frehe, Bulletin voor de Nederlandse Dominikanen, jaargang 2 nr. 6. Uitgave Dominicaans Provincialaat, 11 mei 1967, Nijmegen

Catechism of the Catholic Church (2000). English translation. Rome: Libreria Editrice Vaticana. ISBN 1-57455-110-8

Connell, Janice T. (2007). The Visions of the Children: The Apparitions of the Blessed Mother at Medjugorje. New York: St. Martin's Press. ISBN 0-312-36197-1

El-Fers, M. (2009). Lourdes. Morrisville. ISBN 978-1-4092-9296-8

Ernst Robert, (1957). Die marianischen Botschaften von Amsterdam

Franken, Rudo priest (1998). Hernia. Roggel/Neer: Franken.

Franken, Rudo priest (1999). A journey to Medjugorje. Hilversum: St.Vaak.

Frehe, J. and Terstroet, L.L. (1959). De boodschappen van de Vrouwe van alle Volkeren. Amsterdam: Comité/Secretariaat VvaV.

Hendriks, Jan (2008). Maria, Inleiding tot de katholieke leer over de moeder van de Verlosser. Assen: Van Gorcum. ISBN 978-90-2324470-7

Hooft, A.B. van 't (2002). De Vrouwe van alle Volkeren. Berkel-Enschot: Apostolaat voor de Verspreiding van de boodschappen van Jezus en Maria

Hooft, A.B. van 't (2002). Heroldsbach. Berkel-Enschot: Apostolaat voor de Verspreiding van de boodschappen van Jezus en Maria

Johnston, Francis W. (1980). Fatima: the Great Sign. Rockford, Illinois: Tan Books and Publishers. ISBN 0-895551-63-2

Katholieke Illustratie (1955). O.L. Vrouw van Alle Volkeren, 16 juli 1955

Klos, P.J. (1994) De Vrouwe van alle Volkeren die eens Maria was. Amsterdam: Stg. Vox Populi Dei

Klug, Ignaz (1939. Het katholieke geloof. Een apologetisch, dogmatisch kerkhistorisch overzicht, met een voorwoord van Mgr. J. de Jong, voor Nederland speciaal bewerkt door K. Steur, H.J. van Deursen en H.J. Wachters. Heemstede: De Toorts

Knuvelder, Louis (1958). De Vrouwe van alle Volkeren. Amsterdam: Knuvelder

Knuvelder, Dr. Louis. (1959). Maria en de verschijningen te Amsterdam. The Hague: Pax

Knuvelder, Louis (1969). De geschiedenis van de Vrouwe van Alle Volkeren. Amsterdam: Internationale Werkgemeenschap Vrouwe VAV

Knuvelder, Louis. (1970). L'Histoire de la Dame de tous les Peuples. Amsterdam

Kruk, Ester (2004) Zoals sneeuwvlokjes over de wereld dwarrelen. Amsterdam: Aksant ISBN 90-5260-090-2

Künzli, Josef ed. (1987). Eucharistic experiences, translated from the Dutch. Jestetten: Miriam-Verlag

Leechburch Auwers, J.A.A. (2002). Zie, van nu af aan zullen alle geslachten mij zalig prijzen: Bulletin 02034, The Hague: De Lamp

Lemm, Robert (2003). De Vrouwe van alle Volkeren. Soesterberg: Aspekt. ISBN 978-90-5911216-2

Lemm, Robert (2007). Paus Benedictus XVI en de opkomst van Eurabia. Soesterberg: Aspekt. ISBN 978-90-5911517-0

Lemm, Robert (2008). Maria, haar geheime evangelie. Soesterberg, Aspekt. ISBN 978-90-59113954

Lierde, Mgr Dr P.C. van (1954). Achter de Bronzen Poort. Haarlem: De Toorts

Liesting, dr G.Th.H. S.S.S. (1974). Het zal met de jaren uitkomen. 2nd Print, Comité 'Vrouwe van alle Volkeren', Amsterdam

McClure, Kevin (1983). The Evidence for Visions of the Virgin Mary. Wellingborough: Aquarian Press. ISBN 0-85030-351-6

Nieuwe Revu, nr. 43 (1971)

N.N. (1964). Rozegeur en maneschijn. Een geurige geschiedenis, uitg. t.g.v. het 175-jarig bestaan van de Eau de Colognefabriek: J.C. Boldoot, Amsterdam

Odell, Catherine M. (1995). Those Who Saw Her: Apparitions of Mary. Huntington: Our Sunday Visitor. ISBN 0-87973-664-4

Peerdeman, Ida (1988). De boodschappen van de Vrouwe van alle Volkeren (Dutch edition of the Messages of the Lady of all Nations). Amsterdam. ISBN 3874-49194-3

Peerdeman, Ida (1992). Eucharistische Belevenissen (reprint 1992 of the Dutch original of the of the Eucharistic Experiences). Amsterdam: Stichting Secretariaat Vrouwe van alle Volkeren. ISBN 3-87449-230-3

Peeters, Jan (7-6-1996). Mgr. Bomers doet "mededeling" over "Vrouwe van ale volkeren". Eindhoven: Katholiek Nieuwsblad

Ratzinger, Joseph (2007). Life in the Church and Living Theology: Fundamentals of Ecclesiology. Ft. Collins: Ignatius Press. ISBN 13-9781-5861-7149-0

Ratzinger, Joseph (2009). Maria, Pope Benedict XVI on the Mother of God. Ignatius Press. ISBN 9781-5861-7307-4

Author: Pope Benedict XVI

Refoulé, F. (1969). Au bord du schisme? L'affaire d'Amsterdam et l'Église de Hollande. Paris: Cerf

Reynolds, A.H. (1974) Introducing to the Lady of all Nations

Run, H. van (4-4-1970). Herdenking van de eerste verschijning. Amsterdam: Vrij Nederland

Shimura, Tatsuya (1984). De Heilige Maagd Maria weent in Japan (Akita) Nijmegen: Recht zonder onderscheid

Sigl, Paul Maria (2005). Ida Peerdeman, de Zieneres van Amsterdam. Amsterdam: PDF-Familie van Maria Medeverlosseres. ISBN 3-9521553-6-5.

Sparrow, G. Scott (2004). Sacred Encounters with Mary. Chicago: Thomas More Association/Ave Maria Press. ISBN 1-59471-047-3

Stheeman, Liesbeth (28-3-1970. Waarom moest juist ik Maria zien verschijnen? Amsterdam: De Telegraaf

Voets, B. (1981). Bewaar het toevertrouwde pand. Hilversum: Gooi en Sticht.ISBN 90-304-0212-1

Waterinckx, Mark (2002). Petition. Hilversum: St. Vaak.

Weiguni, Bettina (2005). Die geheimnisvollen Herren von C&A. Frankfurt am Main: Eichborn Verlag. ISBN 3-8218-5600-9

Printed in Great Britain
by Amazon

32452981R00096